David Hume's
ARGUMENT
AGAINST
MIRACLES

A Critical Analysis

Francis J. Beckwith
Department of Philosophy
University of Nevada, Las Vegas

UNIVERSITY
PRESS OF
AMERICA

Lanham • New York • London

Copyright © 1989 by

University Press of America,® Inc.

4720 Boston Way
Lanham, MD 20706

3 Henrietta Street
London WC2E 8LU England

British Cataloging in Publication Information Available

Library of Congress Cataloging-in-Publication Data

Beckwith, Francis.
David Hume's argument against miracles : a critical analysis / Francis J. Beckwith.
        p.   cm.
Bibliography: p.
Includes index.
1. Hume, David, 1711–1776—Views on miracles.   2. Miracles.
3. Apologetics—20th century.   I. Title.
B1499.M5B43   1989   211—dc20   89–33135 CIP

ISBN 0–8191–7487–4 (alk. paper)

#19722107

All University Press of America books are produced on acid-free paper.
The paper used in this publication meets the minimum requirements of American
National Standard for Information Sciences—Permanence of Paper for Printed Library
Materials, ANSI Z39.48–1984.   ∞

DEDICATION

To my grandmother, Frances Guido, who gave me a place to call home during my tenure in New York City. I will be forever grateful.

ACKNOWLEDGEMENTS

I would like to thank the following individuals for their help with the completion of this work: my wife, Frankie R.D. Beckwith, who has lovingly put up with me during my writing frenzy; my Uncle Steve Guido, who gave me the computer on which this text was written; my student and friend, Pastor Barry Diamond of the Vineyard Christian Fellowship of Las Vegas, who permitted me use of his church's printer; my Pastor, David Walker of Christian Life Community Church of Las Vegas, who let me "play with" his church's laser jet printer; Professor Peter Starkweather of UNLV (Biology), who gave me access to his department's printer for the final version of this book; the readers on my dissertation committee, Professors Vincent Cooke, S.J. and James Sadowsky, S.J. (Fordham University), whose thought-provoking questions made necessary the expansion and revision of the dissertation which eventually turned into this book; and last but not least, my dissertation mentor, Professor Robert J. Roth, S.J., who was willing to engage in the trans-continental project from which this book is derived, and whose advice has been priceless. However, I take full and complete responsibility for the contents of this work.

TABLE OF CONTENTS

CHAPTER ONE

INTRODUCTION

In his first letter to the Corinthians the Apostle Paul made the assertion that "if Christ has not been raised then our preaching is useless and your believing it is useless" (15:14). For Paul, the truth of the Christian faith is contingent upon the historicity of the miraculous, and in particular, the miracle of Christ's Resurrection. However, Paul's creedal utterance is certainly not a piece of isolated dogma. The claim that God has acted miraculously in history has been part of the theological arsenal of every major Christian apologist up until the middle of the eighteenth century. Using the example of Christ Himself, Who stated that His claims would be verified by "the sign of the prophet Jonah" (Matthew 12:39,40--namely, His own miraculous Resurrection), the patristic apologists (Irenaeus and Origen, in particular), in line with the Pauline tradition, defended their beliefs by appealing to what they considered to be historically verifiable occurrences of miracles.[1] This tradition continued under the auspices of such diverse Christian thinkers as Augustine, Hugo Grotius, Blaise Pascal, William Paley, and Joseph Butler, to name just a few.[2]

This line of tradition was altered by David Hume's classic philosophical attack, "Of Miracles," in which the Scotsman attempts to demolish the use of miracles as apologetic evidence.[3] Because of what J.K.S. Reid calls "its devastating character," Hume's essay provoked Christian philosophers and theologians to reexamine their apologetic strategy, creating "a movement away from presenting prophecy and miracle as external proofs. . ."[4] To say that Hume's essay made an impact in the history of philosophical and religious thought is, to say the least, an understatement. John Herman Randall, Jr., calling Hume's argument the *"coup de grace,"* has asserted that Hume "has proved so conclusively that intelligent men have rarely questioned, that a miracle, in the sense of a supernatural event as a sign of the divinity of its worker, cannot possibly be established."[5] Elsewhere Randall writes that "since Hume's critique of miracles in the eighteenth century, religious liberals have refused to believe in any such interferences with the order of natural law. . . In the eighteenth century, miracles were the chief support of faith; in the next, they became the chief problem to be explained."[6] American theologians Lawrence Burkholder and Harvey Cox point to Hume's essay as the primary reason for the rejection of miracles by many twentieth century thinkers.[7]

This is not to say that Hume completely obliterated the use of

1

miracles in the Christian philosophy of religion (one thinks immediately of John Henry Cardinal Newman in the nineteenth century[8], and C.S. Lewis[9] and Richard Swinburne[10] in the twentieth century), rather, he so altered the course of the debate that Christian philosophers and theologians, for the most part, have opted for avoiding evidential apologetics altogether.

Although Hume's work on miracles will be the main focus of this book, it is also my intention to address the broader question of the possibility of the miraculous. Hence, three particular concerns will be addressed in this work: (1) Hume's argument against the miraculous; (2) The contemporary philosophical attempts to rehabilitate Hume's work; and (3) The epistemological problems associated with the concept of miracle.

In chapter 2 I will present what I believe is a good working definition of the miraculous. Chapters 3 and 4 will consist of a critical examination of Hume's argument. Hume's attack on the miraculous was a two-pronged effort. The section of his *Enquiry Concerning Human Understanding*, which contains this argument (chapter X), consists of two parts. In Part I, Hume argues *a priori*, concluding that by their very nature miracles cannot be known historically. I call this the *in-principle* argument: miracles in principle cannot be known. Part II consists of criteria set up by Hume to judge the historical evidence of miracles alleged to have happened. I call this the *historical-criteria* argument. As we shall see in our analysis, although there are two parts to Hume's argument, both parts function together in an organic unity. Because of the importance of Hume's theory of knowledge in his rejection of miracles, chapter 3 will deal with both Hume's epistemology and in-principle argument. Chapter 4 will deal with Hume's historical-criteria argument. Since some non-theists argue that one can not say that a miracle is an act of God unless one is already rationally justified in believing that God exists, in Chapter 5 I will discuss the question of whether the believer in miracles is rational in believing in the existence of God.

The anti-miraculous mood in philosophical theology increased from the time of Hume until the twentieth century.[11] But it is not until the latter part of this present century that we find an impressive quantity of philosophically sophisticated defenses of Humean-type arguments. In attempting to defend Hume's position in a contemporary context, a number of philosophers have put forth rehabilitations of Hume's argument.[12] From among these, I have chosen to deal in chapter 5 with the ones I believe are the strongest, as put forth by the following thinkers: Antony Flew,[13] Alastair McKinnon,[14] and Patrick Nowell-Smith.[15]

After the first six chapters of this work the reader will no doubt conclude that the problem of the miraculous is ultimately epistemological. There are essentially two epistemological questions on which the miracles debate rests: (1) Is it ever reasonable to ascribe a divine source to an anomalous event in order to identify it as miraculous?; and (2) What theoretically entails sufficient evidence that a miracle has actually taken place? The former question will be discussed in detail in chapters 4 and 5 when we critique part four of Hume's four-part historical criteria. Chapter 7 will be entirely concerned with the second epistemological question, although much of the philosophical spadework for this chapter will have been completed in chapters 3 and 6. Given our negative appraisal of the naturalist's position in chapters 2-6, I will make some suggestions in chapter 7 as to what direction the believer in miracles should go in showing the historicity of miracle-claims.

NOTES FOR CHAPTER ONE

[1]See *Faith of the Early Fathers*, Vol. 1, ed. William A. Jurgens (Collegeville, Minn.: The Liturgical Press, 1970).

[2]See Avery Dulles, S.J., *A History of Apologetics* (Philadelphia: Westminster, 1971), and Bernard Ramm, *Varieties of Christian Apologetics: An Introduction to the Christian Philosophy of Religion*, rev. ed. (Grand Rapids, Mich.: Baker Book House, 1961)

[3]As contained in David Hume, *An Enquiry Concerning Human Understanding*, 3rd ed., text revised and notes P.H. Nidditch, intro. and analytic index L.A. Selby-Bigge (Oxford: Clarendon, 1975; reprinted from the 1777 edition), pp. 109-131.

[4]J.K.S. Reid, *Christian Apologetics* (London: Hodder & Stoughton, 1969), p. 156

[5]John Herman Randall, Jr., *The Making of the Modern Mind* (New York: Columbia University Press, 1940), p. 293.

[6]*Ibid.*, pp. 553, 554.

[7]Lawrence Burkholder, Harvey Cox, and Wolfhart Pannenberg, "A Dialogue on Christ's Resurrection," *Christianity Today*, 12 (April 12, 1968): 5-12.

[8]John Henry Cardinal Newman, *Two Essays on Biblical and Ecclesiastical Miracles* (Westminster, MD: Christian Classics, 1969)

[9]C.S. Lewis, *Miracles* (Great Britain: Fontana Books, 1947)

[10]Richard Swinburne, *The Concept of Miracle* (New York: Macmillan, 1970)

[11]For a detailed historical summary of this period, see Colin Brown, *Miracles and the Critical Mind* (Grand Rapids, MI: Eerdmans, 1984), pp. 103-277.

[12]When I refer to these arguments as "rehabilitations" I am not saying that Hume has been definitively refuted and these contemporary thinkers are trying to rescue him. Rather, I am saying that these thinkers are employing arguments which are contemporary variations of Hume's argument. However, it should be noted that only Antony Flew, in putting forth his own argument against the miraculous, overtly takes into consideration what he calls "two major and several lesser flaws" in Hume's argument. See Antony Flew in *Did Jesus Rise From the Dead?: The Resurrection Debate*, ed. Terry L. Miethe (New York: Harper & Row, 1987), p. 4. Flew

also makes mention of these flaws in other works; see especially Flew's critique of Hume's view of natural law in his *Hume's Theory of Belief* (London: Routledge and Kegan Paul, 1961), pp. 204-208, which has recently been republished as "Scientific Versus Historical Evidence," in *Miracles*, ed. Richard Swinburne (New York: Macmillan, 1989), pp. 97-102.

[13]Antony Flew, "Miracles," in *Encyclopedia of Philosophy*, Vol. 5, ed. Paul Edwards (New York: Macmillan & The Free Press, 1967), pp. 346-353; Antony Flew, "Parapsychology Revisited: Laws, Miracles, and Repeatability," in *Philosophy and Parapsychology*, ed. Jan Ludwig (Buffalo, NY: Prometheus Books, 1978), pp. 263-269; Antony Flew, *God: A Critical Enquiry*, 2nd ed. (LaSalle, IL: Open Court, 1984), pp. 134-152; Antony Flew, "The Impossibility of the Miraculous," in *Hume's Philosophy of Religion*, the Sixth James Montgomery Hester Seminar (Winston-Salem, NC: Wake Forest University Press, 1986), pp. 9-32; and Antony Flew in *Did Jesus Rise From the Dead?: The Resurrection Debate*, ed. Terry L. Miethe (New York: Harper & Row, 1987)

[14]Alastair McKinnon, "'Miracle' and 'Paradox'," in *American Philosophical Quarterly* 4 (October, 1967): 308-314.

[15]Patrick Nowell-Smith, "Miracles," in *New Essays in Philosophical Theology*, eds. Antony Flew and Alasdair MacIntyre (New York: Macmillan, 1955), pp. 243-253.

CHAPTER TWO

DEFINING THE MIRACULOUS

"What do you mean by the term 'miracle'?" is quite possibly the most important question asked in the current debate. After all, in common parlance the term "miracle" is thrown about in such a manner as to include everything from improbable sports achievements (e.g., the 1969 New York Mets) to beating rush-hour traffic in record time (e.g., "It's a miracle you made it here so quickly"). In fact, after taking a look at a photograph of my wife, a colleague of mine made the observation that it is indeed a "miracle" that such a beautiful woman would marry me. Although there are many popular connotations which the term "miracle" provokes, it is necessary that the term be carefully defined philosophically.

Hume defined a miracle as "a violation of the laws of nature. . ., *a transgression of a law of nature by a particular volition of the Deity, or by the interposition of some invisible agent.*"[1] Although I agree with this definition to a certain extent, it fails to take into consideration an important element in evaluating miraculous events, namely, the historical-religious context surrounding the event (which would include its existential and teleological significance). For this reason, the following is put forth as a broad definition of what I believe most religious people generally mean when they call an event miraculous: *A miracle is a divine intervention which occurs contrary to the regular course of nature within a significant historical-religious context.* This definition can be broken down to entail the following three propositions: (1) *A miracle is rationally inexplicable by scientific law*; (2) *A miracle occurs within a significant historical-religious context*; and (3) *A miracle is an event for which a 'god' is responsible.*[2] In order for any event to be miraculous, all three elements must be present. That is, if any event which is claimed to be miraculous lacks any one of these elements, it is disqualified as a miraculous event. Let us take a closer a look at each one of these elements.

MIRACLES ARE RATIONALLY INEXPLICABLE BY SCIENTIFIC LAWS

What is thought of as "scientific law" is really just what is descriptive of how the universe *regularly* functions based on predictive success.[3] Hence one is incapable, because of the strong anomalous nature of an alleged miraculous event (that is, it is non-analogous and

7

singular), to find a scientific law under which this event can be subsumed. As Swinburne writes:

> To say that a certain such formula is a law is to say that in general its predictions are true and that any exceptions to its operation cannot be accounted for by another formula which could be taken as a law. . . [I]t is clearly a coherent way of talking, and it is the way adopted by those who talk of violations of natural laws. . . If, as seems natural, we understand by the physically impossible what is ruled out by a law of nature, then our account of the laws of nature suggests that it makes sense to suppose that on occasion the physically impossible occurs.[4]

For example, our general experience of human physiology tells us that when a human being has been dead for a number of days, it is physiologically impossible for that individual to eat breakfast and enter into a discussion on eschatology. Therefore, if an individual, several days after he has died, is seen alive having a meal and conversing with friends about the end of the world, then such an event is one which is rationally inexplicable by our scientific laws about how the universe regularly functions.

However, two important distinctions should be made. First, our definition should be distinguished from a recurring scientific anomaly, such as Isaac Newton's observation that some planets have perturbed orbits. A violation of natural law is unique and non-analogous, a recurring anomaly is regular, but inexplicable in terms of current law, although its recurrence points toward the very real possibility of a new law (or a refinement of the old law) under which it can be subsumed.[5] Newton tried to explain his astronomical anomaly by postulating a divine force, and by doing so fell into a God-of-the-gaps procedure: whatever cannot be explained naturally must have a divine source. This is *not* what is being argued for in this book.

Second, our definition should be distinguished from healings and other paranormal phenomena which can be accounted for psychosomatically or by other natural forces. Bryan Van Dragt writes that "studies in such areas as biofeedback and meditation have demonstrated the mind's ability to influence bodily function." For example, "Simonton's cancer research suggests that visual imagery and positive changes in attitude can alter the course of illness, even to the point of total remission of cancer symptoms." But "what is known of psychosomatics fails to account for the rare but well-documented cases of instantaneous and total cure of diseases otherwise thought to be incurable and the rejuvenation of organ systems thought to be beyond repair."[6] The law-violating phenomena one finds in the Bible, such as levitations, resurrections, and the altering of nature by vocal commands (e.g., Moses' splitting of the Red Sea), are events which I would also classify as scientifically inexplicable.

When I talk of scientific inexplicability, I do *not* mean *permanent* scientific inexplicability. For this reason, a couple of comments should be made about David Basinger's assertion that Swinburne, and most every other Christian philosopher who defends the miraculous, "unjustifiably assumes that we presently know enough about the nature of reality to state with certainty that certain occurrences could never be subsumed under even small scale scientific laws."[7] In other words, Christian philosophers erroneously defend a miracle as a *permanent* scientific inexplicability. Apart from the fact that this accusation is a total misreading of Swinburne's position,[8] Basinger is attacking a straw-man. As far as I know, no Christian philosopher of religion or theologian, with the exception of Basinger himself,[9] defines a miracle as permanently inexplicable. The Christian thinkers who have written about miracles most often define a miracle as a singular non-analogous event which is inexplicable in terms of *what we know about currently well-established scientific laws*. As Swinburne points out, although "all claims about what are the laws of nature are corrigible. . . we must reach provisional conclusions about them on the evidence available to us." But the fact of the matter is that "we have to some extent good evidence about what are the laws of nature," and if these laws were allegedly violated, "in such cases the evidence is strong that if the purported counter-instance occurred [i.e.,the miracle] it was a violation of the law of nature."[10] Hence, the fact that one cannot find deductive validity for any scientific law only means that our judgments about events purporting to violate these laws cannot reach the point of apodictic certainty. Since no discipline dealing with empirical judgments can render such certainty (e.g., law, history, psychology, anthropology, archaeology, etc.), it should not bother the believer in miracles one bit that miracles cannot be demonstrated to be permanently inexplicable; scientific inexplicability in terms of currently well-established laws will do just fine.

This clarification, however, will not suffice for Basinger. He writes that "given the proven capacity of the scientific enterprise to generate explanations for states of affairs which were once considered inexplicable, the proponent of this view must acknowledge that occurrences which he now considers miraculous may need to be stripped of that title at some time in the future."[11] And since permanent scientific inexplicability, according to Basinger, is a *necessary* and *sufficient* condition for attributing an event's occurrence to God's handiwork,[12] the Christian theist is never within his epistemic rights to say that God is responsible for a scientifically inexplicable event. There are at least two problems with Basinger's observation. (1) Most theists, as far as I know, claim that the scientific inexplicability of an event (whether or not it is permanent) is not at all a *sufficient* condition to call any event miraculous. After all, one can envision a scientifically

9

inexplicable event which is not considered miraculous because of its lack of a significant historical-religious context (e.g., a snow storm in 100 degree weather in Las Vegas in July). Although scientific inexplicability is a *necessary* condition for any event to be called miraculous, it is certainly not a sufficient condition.[13] As I pointed out above, there are three necessary conditions that would make an event miraculous, none of which individually is a sufficient condition. Hence, scientific inexplicability (whether permanent or not) is insufficient in identifying direct acts of God apart from the truth of the two other necessary conditions (see below for a detailed presentation of these conditions).

(2) One can question with good reason the claim underlying Basinger's argument, namely, that if an event is *not* a permanent scientific inexplicability it cannot be used "to identify direct acts of God"[14] because it is always possible--"given the proven capacity of the scientific enterprise"--that there could someday be a scientific explanation of the event. First, as I have written above, since other disciplines do not function within the confines of apodictic certainty (e.g., law, anthropology, archaeology, etc.), it is unreasonable to ask the Christian theist to prove the permanent scientific inexplicability of an event in order to help identify this event as a direct act of God. Could not the Christian theist say that it is reasonable to believe an event is miraculous because it violates well-established laws, and yet be willing to change his view in light of a new scientific theory which explains the event? On Basinger's rationale, it would always be unreasonable for a jury to convict a man on the basis of well-established evidence because it is always possible that more evidence could turn up that would invalidate the well-established evidence.

Second, it should be noted that science's problem-solving capacity has been completely impotent in making *any* of the primary law-violating miracles of the Christian tradition scientifically explicable, e.g., resurrections, changing water into wine, walking through walls, levitating, multiplying fishes and loaves, instantaneously healing lepers, and walking on water. As Gary R. Habermas has pointed out:

> . . . [A]s several philosophers and apologists have argued, certain rare miracle-claims are not only presently inexplicable, but the laws appear to have no explanatory power in the future. For instance, cancer is the sort of thing for which we *would* expect to find a cure in the future, whereas the resurrection of Jesus in a glorified body would be much more troublesome to the naturalist not only in that it is presently inexplicable but in that we have no hints how it could ever be explained.[15]

Granted it is *possible* a scientific explanation for these

occurrences will be discovered, the fact that science has not found *any* explanation, and has not even come close, should count for something. That is, given science's proven *incapacity* to generate natural scientific explanations of *these* occurrences (and given the truth of the other two necessary conditions), I cannot see why it would be unreasonable on the part of the believer in miracles to assert that he has good reason to believe these occurrences have been brought about by a non-natural entity. To appeal to a possible future in which they are scientifically explicable is simply to beg the question in favor of naturalism.

Although an event which is scientifically inexplicable may very well be a miracle, the following two elements must be present for it to be accurately described as such.

MIRACLES OCCUR WITHIN A SIGNIFICANT HISTORICAL-RELIGIOUS CONTEXT

There is a direct correlation between the event itself and the context in which the event occurs. Although writing about religious language, Jerry Gill's comments are applicable concerning this point:

> To attempt to analyze meaning apart from context, convention, and intentions, as critical philosophers generally do, will inevitably distort both the meaning of a given utterance and one's understanding of meaning in general.[16]

Miracles are not just purposeless and bizarre scientific oddities, but occur in such a way that purpose is attached to them by virtue of when and why they occur. For example, in the case of the individual who was seen alive eating and talking a number of days after he had died, imagine that he had attached certain theological truth-claims about himself to his ability to perform the physiologically impossible, to convincingly defeat death (that is to say, if he defeats death, then his claims are true). Furthermore, this individual's unparalleled life and teachings, which are said to have culminated in his physical resurrection, had such a profound effect on his disciples that they addressed him as a divine being (quite possibly, God Himself) and dedicated the remaining years of their lives to proclaiming the truth of his message. Moreover, let us assume that the claims this individual has made about himself had direct implications for the culture in which he lived: the truth of his claims entails that he is the theological fulfillment of what all the esteemed and revered prophets of the past had predicted. Within this religious context the physiological anomaly of a resurrection takes on a significance which would have not been present if this individual had "just happened" to rise from the dead for no apparent reason. That is, the historical-religious context of the event entails

11

the event's existential and teleological significance, which, with the scientific inexplicability of the event, could help us to reasonably infer the event's cause, a god.

MIRACLES ARE BROUGHT ABOUT BY A "GOD"

Accepting Swinburne's definition, we define a "god" in the following way: a god is "a *non-embodied* rational agent of great power."[17] By "non-embodied" I simply mean that this agent possesses no body; "there is no one material object, occurrences affecting which he feels and which he has particularly under his control, to be distinguished from other material objects of which this is not true."[18] By "rational agent" I simply mean a being who possesses the attributes of a person; this being "can reason, choose, decide, intend, has likes and dislikes, is capable of moral or immoral action."[19] When I say that this being has great power I simply "mean that he can produce effects in the world far beyond the powers of men to produce."[20]

It is obvious that I do not *necessarily* mean the God of the Christian tradition, although there is little doubt that the objections of Hume and his contemporary followers are aimed at the miracles within this tradition. I believe that it is too restrictive to define a miracle strictly in terms of the Christian God. After all, other religions, with rival conceptions of God, claim that miracles have been performed by their respective deities. However, this does not mean that it is not more reasonable to believe, on the basis of independent theistic arguments and the quality and actuality of certain miracles, that a particular god is more likely to be the true God.[21]

How one is able to discern the involvement of a god is the main problem which arises when one talks about a god as the active agent in an empirical event. I will argue that one can reasonably infer that a god is the rational agent in bringing about a particular miraculous event (see chapters 4 and 5).

Admittedly, the above definition of the miraculous does not include what some refer to as "second class miracles."[22] Miracles of this sort differ from our definition in this regard: second class miracles *can* be explained in terms of scientific law, but because of their timely occurrence and religious significance they merit the appellation of miracle. R.F. Holland gives us an example of such a miracle:

> A child riding his toy motor-car strays on to an unguarded railway crossing near his house and a wheel of his car gets stuck down the side of one of the rails. An express train is due to pass with the signals in its favor and a curve in the track makes it impossible for the driver to stop his train in time to avoid any obstruction he might encounter on the

crossing. The mother coming out of the house to look for her child sees him on the crossing and hears the train approaching. She runs forward shouting and waving. The little boy remains seated in his car, looking forward, engrossed, in the task of pedaling it free. The brakes of the train are applied and it comes to a rest a few feet from the child. The mother thanks God for the miracle; which she never ceases to think of as such, although, as she in due course learns, there was nothing supernatural about the manner in which the brakes of the train came to be applied. The driver had fainted, for a reason which had nothing to do with the presence of the child on the line, and the brakes were applied automatically as his hand ceased to exert pressure on the control lever.[23]

Though I do not doubt that such an occurrence may merit the appellation of miraculous within the confines of a particular religious tradition, the purpose of this book is to examine objections to the miraculous found in the broadly defined Humean tradition. Since a critical examination of second class miracles does not appear in the works we will discuss, I will not touch upon this topic.

NOTES FOR CHAPTER TWO

[1]David Hume, *An Enquiry Concerning Human Understanding*, 3rd ed., text revised and notes P.H. Nidditch, intro. and analytic index L.A. Selby-Bigge (Oxford: Clarendon, 1975; reprinted from the 1777 edition), pp. 114-115. It should be noted that Hume understood scientific law in the sense that it was understood in his day, i.e., as being strictly determined and prescriptive. However, it is against this version that he reacted, arguing that necessary connection could not be philosophically validated. He thus rejected scientific laws as then understood, or at least argued that we could not justify them philosophically. Hume claimed that a natural law is based on *uniform* experience. And since a miracle is defined as a violation of natural law, the actuality of a miracle counts against the uniform experience on which the law is based. Therefore, since you cannot have a miracle without law, any argument for miracles collapses. See chapter 3 for a fuller explanation of Hume's view of natural law and miracles.

[2]This definition of the miraculous is similar to ones put forth by William Lane Craig and Richard Swinburne. Craig defines a miracle as an event which so "exceeds what we know of natural causes that it seems most reasonable to attribute it to a supernatural cause," and "the religio-historical context furnishes us with the key to the supernatural character of that event." (William Lane Craig, *Apologetics: An Introduction* [Chicago: Moody Press, 1984], pp. 119-120). Swinburne defines a miracle in the following way: "To start with we may say very generally that a miracle is an event of an extraordinary kind, brought about by a god, and of religious significance." (Richard Swinburne, *The Concept of Miracle* [New York: Macmillan, 1970], p. 1).

[3]It should be noted that "scientific law" as descriptive and predictive is the contemporary view, not the *prescriptive* view of the 18th and 19th centuries; a view that Hume himself was reacting against. Therefore, when a contemporary scientist calls something a "scientific law" he is not saying that such a law rigidly *prescribes* what must happen a priori (e.g., "Miracles never happen because nature is, by definition, unalterable,"), rather, he is *describing* how the universe regularly functions in terms of the predictive success of certain scientific laws. The upshot of this is that a *descriptive* view of natural law cannot rule out the actuality of miracles *a priori*. For this reason, the German physicist Werner Schaaffs acknowledges that "even the physicist must officially concede the possibility of intervention by God." (Werner Schaafs, *Theology, Physics, and Miracles* [Washington, D.C.: Canon Press, 1974], p. 66). See also, Mary Hesse, "Miracles and the Laws of Nature," in *Miracles*, ed. C.F.D. Moule (London: A.R. Mowbray, 1965)

[4]Swinburne, *Concept*, p. 27-28.

[5]Larry Laudan cites the following example: "The process of converting anomalies (real or apparent) into solved problems is as old as science itself; the history of ancient astronomy is replete with examples of it. Indeed, the basic idea is encapsulated in the classic aphorism *exceptio probat regulam*--which originally meant that a rule or principle is tested by its ability to deal with its apparent exceptions. Although numerous examples of this conversion phenomenon could be cited, the best known is probably Prout's hypothesis concerning atomic composition. It was Prout's view that all the elements were composed of hydrogen and, consequently, the atomic weights of all elements should be integral multiples of the weight of hydrogen. Shortly after the appearance of this doctrine in 1815, numerous chemists pointed to seeming exceptions or anomalies. Berzelius and others found that several elements had atomic weights incompatible with Prout's. . . These results constituted very serious anomalies for Proutian chemists. By the beginning of the twentieth century, however, the discovery of isotopes and the refinement of techniques of isotopic separation enabled physical chemists to separate out the isotopes of the same element; each isotope was found to have an atomic weight which was an integral multiple of hydrogen. The previously anomalous results could now be explained on Prout's hypothesis by showing them to be isotopic mixtures. Thus, *the very phenomena which had earlier constituted anomalies for Prout's hypothesis became positive instances of it.* Almost every major theory in the history of science has been able to produce comparable successes at digesting some of its initial anomalies." (Larry Laudan, *Progress and Its Problems: Towards a Theory of Scientific Growth* [Berkeley, CA: University of California Press, 1977], pp. 30-31).

[6]Bryan Van Dragt, "Faith Healing," in *Psychology and Religion*, ed. David G. Benner (Grand Rapids, MI: Baker Book House, 1988), p. 49. See R. Clapp, "Faith Healing: A Look at What's Happening," *Christianity Today* 27 (1983): 12-17, and O.C. Simonton, S. Matthews-Simonton, and J. Creighton, *Getting Well Again* (Los Angeles: J.P. Tarcher, 1978). See also Leon Pearl's explanation of the differences between what he believes are three different types of scientific anomalies in his "Miracles: The Case For Theism," *American Philosophical Quarterly*, 25 (October 1988): 331-337.

[7]David Basinger, "Christian Theism and the Concept of Miracle: Some Epistemological Perplexities," *Southern Journal of Philosophy*, 18 (1980): 141.

[8]In contradiction to Basinger's reading of his position, Swinburne writes: "All claims about what are the laws of nature are corrigible. However much support any purported law has at the moment, on day it may

prove to be no true law. So likewise will be all claims about what does or does not violate the laws of nature. When an event apparently violates such laws, the appearance may arise simply because no one has thought of the true law which could explain the event, or, while they have thought of it, it is so complex relative to the data as rightly to be dismissed before being tested, or too complex to be adopted without further testing and the tests too difficult in practice to carry out. New scientific knowledge may later turn up which forces us to revise any such claims about what violates laws of nature." (Swinburne, *Concept*, pp. 31-32).

[9]Although Basinger argues that permanent inexplicability is untenable in his article, "Christian Theism and the Concept of Miracle," he argues in a later piece ("Miracles as Violations: Some Clarifications," *Southern Journal of Philosophy* 22 [1984]: 1-7) that "it would be useful for theologians and philosophers to refrain from defining miracles as violations of natural laws and define them rather as permanently inexplicable or coincidental direct acts of God. Severe epistemological problems would remain. But most of the traditional conceptual criticisms of the miraculous could be avoided." (*Ibid.*, p. 7). He seems to be advocating what he earlier wrote was epistemologically doomed. His reason for opting for permanent inexplicability rather than the violation concept is that he believes the latter is only coherent within a non-theistic framework; "an event can only be said to violate a law for only one reason: because what 'always' happens under a given set of natural conditions did not happen under this exact set of natural conditions." (*Ibid.*, p. 6). That is, if God is predicated to explain a given violation-event, there is then no "exact set of natural conditions" because God's presence in the explanation changes these "natural conditions". Of course, this whole distinction hinges on the meaning of the term "natural". If one defines natural as that which is finite, created, and non-supernatural, I don't see how the factor of God's presence in an event would alter the set of *natural* conditions. However, for the sake of clarity, I define a "violation of natural law" as synonymous with that which is "scientifically inexplicable." As to whether *permanent inexplicability* is a viable option for the believer in miracles, I refer the reader to the discussion in the text.

[10]Swinburne, *Concept*, pp. 31-32.

[11]Basinger, "Christian Theism," p. 148.

[12]*Ibid.*, pp. 138-142.

[13]Robert Baum writes that a "necessary condition. . .is one in the absence of which the event *cannot* take place. A sufficient condition is

16

one in the presence of which the event is *certain* to take place." (Robert Baum, *Logic*, 2nd edition [New York: Holt, Rhinehart and Winston, 1981], p. 499). In our definition of the miraculous, the sufficient condition is the *conjunction of all the necessary conditions*: if necessary conditions X, Y, and Z obtain together in event M, then M is a miracle.

[14]Basinger, "Christian Theism," p. 141.

[15]Gary R. Habermas, "Miracles Revisited: A Response to Basinger and Basinger," p. 5. Paper presented at the 39th annual meeting of the Evangelical Theological Society (December 3-5, 1987), Gordon-Conwell Theological Seminary, South Hamilton, Massachusetts.

[16]Jerry Gill, *On Knowing God* (Philadelphia: Westminster, 1981), p. 82.

[17]Swinburne, *Concept*, p. 6

[18]*Ibid*

[19]*Ibid*. Of course, if one has a concept of a god which entails that this god is all-perfect and all-powerful, it would be logically impossible for this being to perform an immoral act. As Thomas Aquinas has pointed out, "To sin is to fall short of a perfect action; hence to be able to sin is to be able to fall short in action, which is repugnant to omnipotence. Therefore it is that God cannot sin, because of his omnipotence." (Thomas Aquinas, *Summa Theologica*, I, 25, 3, as found in *Introduction to Saint Thomas Aquinas*, ed. and intro. Anton C. Pegis [New York: The Modern Library, 1948], p. 231). Since we have not shown why it is reasonable to believe that such a god is responsible for any miracle, we must be open to the possibility of a god who is a rational agent capable of performing an immoral act.

[20]Swinburne, *Concept*, p. 6.

[21]For example, some Christian philosophers of religion argue for the reasonableness of the assertion that the Christian God is the only true God, because they believe it has been verified by Jesus' Resurrection, a miracle which is (1) the qualitatively best miracle and (2) unrivaled by the alleged miracles of other religions in its evidential foundation. In addition to their own unique contributions to the miracles debate, the following thinkers each argue for one or both of the above points: William Lane Craig, *Apologetics*, pp. 124-125; Norman L. Geisler, *Christian Apologetics* (Grand Rapids, MI: Baker Book House, 1976), pp. 275-276; Norman L. Geisler, *Miracles and Modern Thought* (Grand Rapids, MI: Zondervan, 1982), pp. 140, 152; Gary R. Habermas, "Skepticism: Hume," in *Biblical Errancy: An Analysis of Its Philosophical Roots*, ed.

Norman L. Geisler (Grand Rapids, MI: Zondervan, 1981), pp. 41-42; and John Warwick Montgomery, "Science, Theology, and The Miraculous," in his *Faith Founded on Fact* (New York: Thomas Nelson, 1978), pp. 61-62.

[22]For example, philosophers Norman L. Geisler (*Christian Apologetics*, pp. 276-279) and R.F. Holland ("The Miraculous," in *Logical Analysis and Contemporary Theism*, ed. John Donnelly [New York: Fordham University Press, 1972], pp. 218-235) defend the concept of a second class miracle, although Holland refers to it as the *contingency concept* of miracle (*Ibid.*, p. 221).

[23]Holland, "The Miraculous," p. 219.

CHAPTER THREE

HUME'S ARGUMENT, PART 1:
EPISTEMOLOGY AND THE IN-PRINCIPLE ARGUMENT

In order to fully grasp Hume's argument against miracles, it is necessary that one come to grips with the epistemological foundation set forth in the text in which this argument is contained, *An Enquiry Concerning Human Understanding.*[1] The following does not pretend to be an exhaustive presentation of Hume's epistemology, but rather it is a summary of those aspects which are important in understanding his argument against miracles.

HUME'S EPISTEMOLOGY

Hume developed his epistemology within the philosophical tradition broadly defined as British Empiricism. This school of thought has its origin in the writings of Francis Bacon,[2] and received further development in the works of John Locke[3] and George Berkeley.[4] Although the empiricists disagreed with each other on several different points, they did agree on the primary principle of empiricism: all knowledge begins with sense experience.

Impressions and Ideas

Hume's empiricism teaches that the content of consciousness consists of perceptions. Perceptions are either *impressions* or *ideas*. *Impressions* are our immediate sensations, passions and emotions; they are the immediate data of touching, hearing, seeing, loving, and hating. *Ideas* are faint images or copies of our impressions, those perceptions we have when we recall our immediate impressions. According to Hume, "impressions are distinguished from ideas, which are the less lively perceptions, of which we are conscious, when we reflect on any of those sensations or movements above mentioned."[5]

Although not as strongly stated in the *Enquiry* as in his *Treatise of Human Nature*, Hume further divides perceptions into *simple and complex impressions* and *simple and complex ideas.*[6] According to Hume, "simple perceptions or impressions and ideas are such as admit of no distinction nor separation." On the other hand, "the complex are the contrary to these, and may be distinguished into parts."[7] That is to say, complex impressions and complex ideas can be reduced to irreducible simple impressions and simple ideas. Ultimately, however, all knowledge is derived from simple impressions, although in one place Hume acknowledges the legitimacy of inferring *from* sense experience an entity not found *in* sense experience.[8]

An example of a complex impression would be the immediate perception of an apple. This complex impression can be divided into simple impressions, such as redness (color), roundness (shape), tartness (taste), etc. And, quite naturally, the complex idea of an apple can be said to consist of simple ideas which correspond to the appropriate simple impressions.

The main point which Hume is trying put across is that we cannot know anything of which we have not had a prior impression in sensory experience. Even in our religious dreams of a New Jerusalem or in the science fiction tales of the Star Ship Enterprise, we cannot imagine anything which is not ultimately reducible to sensory experience. For that which is imaginative, such as the complex idea of a New Jerusalem, can be broken down into simple ideas (e.g., gold, walls, rubies, etc.), which are derived from simple impressions, out of which the mind has formed this imaginative complex idea.[9]

Matters of Fact and Relations of Ideas

Given that all knowledge is derived from sense experience, Hume concluded that "all the objects of human reason and enquiry may naturally be divided into two kinds, to wit, *Relations of Ideas*, and *Matters of Fact*."[10] The latter can be defined as simply those propositions which refer to empirical perceptions. Matters of fact have no necessity. In other words, there is no contradiction in conceiving the opposite of a matter of fact. As Hume puts it, "The contrary of every matter of fact is still possible; because it can never imply a contradiction, and is conceived by the mind with the same facility and distinctness, as if ever so conformable to reality." He goes on to say, "*That the sun will not rise to-morrow* is no less intelligent a proposition, and implies no more contradiction, than the affirmation, *that it will rise.* We should in vain, therefore, attempt to demonstrate its falsehood." That is to say, "were it demonstratively false, it would imply a contradiction, and could never be distinctively conceived by the mind."[11]

On the other hand, relations of ideas refer to certain propositions which are formally true, such as the truths of mathematics, logic, and algebra. They do not refer to any matter of fact, and are tautological (true by definition). For example, $2+2=4$ is true by definition and is therefore certain; it is strictly a formal truth having to do with no matter of fact. Furthermore, one cannot, without contradiction, deny a proposition which is a relation of ideas. Unlike a matter of fact, the

20

contrary of a relation of ideas is inconceivable. For example, without contradicting oneself, one can imagine a world in which David Hume was never born. However, one would be caught in a contradiction if one were to try to imagine that $2+2=5$. "Propositions of this kind are discoverable by the mere operation of thought, without dependence on what is any where existent in the universe."[12] Since knowledge is reducible to two types of propositions, Hume concludes his *Enquiry* with the following appraisal of theological and metaphysical truth-claims:

> When we run over libraries, persuaded of these principles, what havoc must we make? If we take in our hand any volume--of divinity or school metaphysics, for instance--let us ask, *Does it contain any abstract reasoning concerning quantity or number?* No. *Does it contain any experimental reasoning concerning matter of fact and existence?* No. Commit it then to the flames, for it can contain nothing but sophistry and illusion.[13]

Causality and Constant Conjunction

Another important aspect of Hume's epistemology is his analysis of causality concerning matters of fact. According to Hume, "all reasonings concerning matter of fact seem to be founded on the relation of *Cause and Effect*. By means of that relation alone we can go beyond the evidence of our memory and senses."[14] Since one can imagine, without involving a logical contradiction, two matters of fact in a causal sequence as separate and distinct, Hume concludes that there is an epistemological barrier which prevents one from demonstrating a necessary connection between two events. The mind is incapable of ascertaining the definite cause for a given effect; there is no logically necessary reason why a particular effect should have a particular cause. Hume writes that it is only "after the *constant conjunction* of objects--heat and flame, for instance. . .--[that] we are determined by *custom alone* to expect the one from the appearance from the other" (emphasis mine).[15] Our notion of causality is not derived from any self-evident rational principle, but is *believed* because of a *constant conjunction* of events. We are unable to know *the necessary connection* between any two events, but only what we *customarily* infer from a *constant conjunction*. "All inferences from experience, therefore are effects of custom, not of reasoning."[16]

This notion of causality based on constant conjunction has a definite bearing upon the question of miracles, although it seems that Hume did not recognize this fact.[17] Hume writes that "in vain. . . should we pretend to determine any single event, or infer any cause or effect, without the assistance of observation or experience."[18] Applying this to the miraculous it can be asked: since the cause of a miracle is

21   ↳ Their Point!

said to be a god, and a miracle is a unique event, how is it possible for the believer in miracles to say that a god is responsible for this event? That is to say, there appears to be no constant conjunction of miracles from which such a cause can be inferred. This problem will be dealt with in the chapters 4 and 5.

Probability and Proof

As noted earlier, Hume stated that we cannot be certain that the sun will rise tomorrow. We can only *believe*, out of custom and habit, that it will in fact rise tomorrow as it has always done so in the past. And, of course, "as a great number of views do here concur in one event, they fortify and confirm it to the imagination, beget that sentiment which we call *belief*, and give its object the preference above the contrary event, which is not supported by an equal number of experiments, and recurs not so frequently to the thought in transferring the past to the future."[19] And that which commands our belief by a greater number of experiments than its opposition is that which has more *probability* in its favor. Furthermore, that which has the highest probability in its favor is said to be a *proof*. "By *proofs* meaning such arguments from experience as leave no room for doubt or opposition."[20] Hume writes:

[handwritten margin notes]: credible / A person saying / I saw it out / weighs the 100 / who didn't see / it

> There are some causes, which are entirely uniform and constant in producing a particular effect; and no instance has ever yet been found of any failure or irregularity in their operation [i.e., a proof]. Fire has always burned, water suffocated every human creature: The production of motion by impulse and gravity is an universal law, which has hitherto admitted no exception. . . But where different effects have been found to follow from causes, which are to *appearance* exactly similar, all these various effects must occur to the mind in transferring the past to the future, and enter into our consideration, when we determine the probability of the event. Though we give the preference to that which has been found most usual, and believe that this effect will exist, we must not overlook the other effects, but must assign to each of them a particular weight and authority, in proportion as we have found it to be more or less frequent [i.e., probability]. It is more probable, in almost every country of Europe, that there will be frost sometime in January, than that the weather will continue open throughout the whole month; though this probability varies according to the different climates, and approaches near certainty in the more northern kingdoms.[21]

John V. Price explains how Hume's view of proof and probability fits in with the other elements of his epistemology:

> Knowledge for Hume depends upon two activities of the mind: the impingement of simple impressions upon the senses, and the causal ordering of ideas corresponding to these impressions. Thus, the mind creates a series of inferences which it accepts as true, but at any moment could be falsified. In a rather loose sense, Hume is applying the *post hoc ergo propter hoc* principle of logic to the experience of the human being in a series of events. We may indeed see X precede Y on any number of occasions, but we cannot say that reason teaches us that X causes Y. While we can be relatively sure that the sun will rise every morning, as it has in the past, we express only a probability, not a fact.[22]

As we shall see in our analysis of Hume and miracles, this notion of probability weighs heavily in his epistemological rejection of the miraculous.

HUME'S ARGUMENT AGAINST MIRACLES

Colin Brown points out that "no work on miracles penned in the seventeenth, eighteenth, or nineteenth centuries receives greater attention today than Hume's slim essay."[23] Antony Flew has written that "the Section 'Of Miracles' has probably provoked more polemic than anything else Hume ever wrote."[24] Although these assessments are indisputable, Hume's argument was not exactly original. Arguments similar to Hume's can be found in the writings of Benedict Spinoza[25] and the Deists.[26] In fact, when Hume's essay was first published it was overshadowed by Conyers Middleton's work, *A Free Inquiry into the Miraculous Powers which are Supposed to have Subsisted in the Christian Church, from the Earliest Ages through Several Successive Centuries. . .*[27] But as Brown has observed, "posterity has made more than ample redress" for Hume's temporary obscurity.[28]

However, what did make Hume's essay unique was its unabashed non-theistic non-rationalistic naturalism, something not shared by either his rationalistic or deistic predecessors and contemporaries. Although there is little doubt that his argument against miracles had been influenced by both Spinoza and the Deists, Hume did in fact reject the rationalism of the former[29] and the theistic proofs of the latter.[30] For this reason, in addition to being the best-argued essay on the topic for its time, I believe that Hume's essay is rightfully considered the classic anti-miraculous assault upon Christian theism.

As I pointed out earlier, Hume's attack on the miraculous was a two-pronged effort. In Part I, Hume argues *a priori*, concluding that by their very nature miracles cannot be known historically. I call this the *in-principle* argument: miracles in principle cannot be known. Part II consists of criteria set up by Hume to judge the historical evidence of miracles alleged to have happened. I call this the *historical-criteria* argument. These two arguments overlap to give Hume a powerful case against supernaturalism. William Lane Craig has written that there is an organic unity to Hume's essay, and that "Hume's reasoning takes the form of an 'Even if. . ., but in fact. . . argument."[31] In part I of his essay Hume argues that *even if* there is evidence that in normal circumstances would lead us to believe that an event has occurred, the intelligent person would not do so in the case of an event that is supposedly miraculous. In part II Hume points out that, *but in fact*, no such evidence actually exists for a miracle.

The key to understanding Hume's argument is how he employs his epistemological distinction between proof and probability. In part I Hume assumes, for the sake of argument ("even if. . ."), that there actually is a miracle with enough evidence which would constitute a proof. However, he also argues that the entire human experience of the uniformity of the laws of nature is itself a proof. Therefore, since the proof for natural laws will always be greater than the proof for any particular miracle, "there is proof against proof," and weighing the "probabilities," Hume concludes that the intelligent person will always reject the miraculous.[32] In part II of his essay, Hume attempts to demonstrate that, *in fact*, there has never been good evidence for a miracle which would constitute a full proof (see chapter 4 for an analysis of this part of his argument).

A Presentation of Hume's In-Principle Argument

Hume begins this section of the *Enquiry* with a comparison of his work on miracles with John Tillotson's[33] argument against the Roman Catholic doctrine of transubstantiation. Hume writes that Tillotson's argument "is as concise, and elegant, and strong as any argument can possibly be supposed against a doctrine so little worthy of a serious refutation."[34] Tillotson puts forth his argument in the following way:

> Every man hath as great evidence that transubstantiation is false as he hath that the Christian religion is true. Suppose then transubstantiation to be part of the Christian doctrine, it must then have the same confirmation with the whole, and that is miracles: but, of all the doctrines in the world, it is peculiarly incapable of being proved by a miracle. For if a miracle were wrought for the proof of it, the very same assurance which any man hath of the truth of the miracle, he hath of the falsehood of the doctrine; that is, the clear

24

evidence of his senses. For that there is a miracle wrought to prove that what he sees in the sacrament, is not bread, but the body of Christ, there is only the evidence of sense; and there is the very same evidence to prove, that what he sees in the sacrament, is not the body of Christ, but bread.[35]

Hume's argument is similar in this regard: Tillotson argues that if the truth of the unobservable phenomenon of transubstantiation were dependent on an observable miracle, the evidence for transubstantiation (the observability of the miracle) would actually count against transubstantiation; that is, the reason you believe the miracle (it can be observed) is the same reason why you reject transubstantiation (it can not be observed). In like manner, Hume argues that the reason why you believe an event is miraculous--that it violates natural law--is the same reason why you reject the miraculous: the proof of natural law outweighs the proof of any miracle (as to the possible ways to interpret what Hume means by this, see the critique of his argument in this chapter). Comparing his argument to Tillotson's, Hume writes:

> I flatter myself, that I have discovered an argument of a like nature, which, if just, will, with the wise and learned, be an everlasting check to all kinds of superstitious delusion, and consequently, will be useful as long as the world endures. For so long, I presume, will the accounts of miracles and prodigies be found in all history, sacred and profane.[36]

Reiterating the epistemological framework set forth earlier in the text, Hume goes on to write that experience is "our only guide in reasoning concerning matters of fact," although "this guide is not altogether infallible, but in some cases is apt to lead us into errors." Admitting that "in our reasonings concerning matter of fact, there are all imaginable degrees of assurance," he asserts that "a wise man," nevertheless, "proportions his belief to the evidence." In some cases, a belief may be founded on infallible experience, and the wise man therefore "regards his past experience as a full *proof* of the future existence of that event." However, "in other cases, he proceeds with more caution: He weighs the opposite experiments: He considers which side is supported by the greater number of experiments: to that side he inclines, with doubt and hesitation; and when at last he fixes his judgment, the evidence exceeds not what we properly call *probability*."[37]

Hume then applies this reasoning to the reports of eyewitnesses in general (not only to the alleged eyewitnesses of miracles). He writes that when it comes to human testimony we should not ignore the epistemological principle set forth in the earlier part of the *Enquiry*: "It being a general maxim, that no objects have any discernible connnexion together, and that all the inferences, which we can draw from

25

one to another, are founded merely on our experience of their constant and regular conjunction." Since human testimony "is founded on past experience, so it varies with experience, and is regarded either as a *proof* or a *probability*, according as the conjunction between a particular kind of report and any kind of object has been found to be constant and variable."[38]

According to Hume, whenever we are judging human testimony "we balance the opposite circumstances, which cause any doubt or uncertainty; and when we discover a superiority on any side, we incline to it; but still with a diminution of assurance, in proportion to the force of its antagonist." [39] What he means by this is simply that the human testimony of a particular event may be opposed by a contrariety of evidence (e.g., contradictory testimony, too few witnesses of doubtful character, etc.), "which may diminish or destroy the force of any argument, derived from human testimony."[40] Therefore, an event having strong evidence in its favor and little or no contrary evidence possesses a very high degree of probability.

Prior to applying the above to the miraculous, Hume first applies it to those witnesses who have claimed to have partaken in what he calls "the extraordinary and the marvellous" (today we put in the classification of extraordinary or marvellous such alleged events as visitations by UFO occupants). Hume writes that "the evidence, resulting from the testimony, admits of a diminution, greater or less, in proportion as the fact is more or less unusual." That is to say, "when the fact attested is such a one as has seldom fallen under our observation, here is a contest of two opposite experiences; of which one destroys the other, as far as its force goes, and the superior can only operate on the mind by the force, which remains."[41] Hume is saying that the extraordinary nature of the event counts as contrary evidence against the event having actually happened. To use an example: our overwhelming experience tells us that elephants do not have wings, and therefore cannot fly. However, let us say that two airplane pilots on a rainy, lightening-filled, winter night observe from the cockpit what they perceive to be a flying elephant. According to Hume, we should weigh the pilots' testimony against the contrary evidence of our overwhelming experience of never having observed a flying elephant, and conclude that it is more likely that the pilots were somehow deceived than the fact that a flying elephant was actually observed. "The very same principle of experience, which gives us a certain degree of assurance in the testimony of witnesses [i.e., pilots are trained observers and often accurate], gives us also, in this case, another degree of assurance against the fact, which they endeavor to establish [i.e., flying elephants have never been a part of our experience, but mistaken pilots have]."[42]

Hume now moves from the marvellous to the miraculous. He asks us to imagine that there is testimony for an alleged miracle which "amounts to an entire proof." In other words, as we noted earlier, he is arguing that *even if* there is good evidence for the miraculous we still should not believe that it has occurred. For the regularity of natural law is itself a "proof." Therefore, we weigh proof against proof, and since "a miracle is a violation of the laws of nature" and "a firm and unalterable experience has established these laws, the proof against a miracle, from the very nature of the fact, is as entire as any argument can be imagined."[43] Hume goes on to assert:

> There must, therefore, be a uniform experience against every miraculous event, otherwise the event would not merit that appellation. And as a uniform experience amounts to a proof, there is here a direct and full *proof*, from the nature of the fact, against the existence of any miracle; nor can such a proof be destroyed, or the miracle rendered credible, but by an opposite proof, which is superior.[44]

Take for example the story in the Book of Joshua when the sun stood still for one day while the Amorites were conquered by Israel (Joshua 10:13). According to Hume, Newton's laws of planetary motion (which includes the law that the sun never remains motionless), having been substantiated by a countless number of observations, would serve as contrary evidence to what allegedly happened in the book of Joshua.[45]

Hume recognizes that one of the consequences of his argument is that in principle no testimony is sufficient to establish the veracity of any miraculous event.[46] For example, he tells us that if someone approached him claiming to have witnessed a dead man resurrected to life, Hume would ask himself whether it is more probable that this witness "should either deceive or be deceived, or that the fact, which he relates, should really have happened."[47] And, of course, since it is more probable that the witness is a victim of some sort of deception than the fact that a resurrection had actually occurred, Hume would reject the miracle. As he puts it: "If the falsehood of his [the witness'] testimony would be more miraculous, than the event which he relates; then, and not till then, can he pretend to command my belief or opinion."[48] Therefore, "since the wise man. . . proportions his belief to the evidence,"[49] one should not believe that a miracle has occurred. Hume's in-principle argument can be summarized in the following argument-outline:

1. Natural laws are built on uniform experience (which, according to Hume, is what makes something a "proof").

2. Miracles are alleged violations of natural law (and are therefore rare).

3. Therefore, the "proof" of natural laws always outweighs the "proof" of any particular miracle.

4. The wise person should always choose to believe that which has the greater weight of evidence.

5. Therefore, miracles can never be believed by a wise person.

A Critique of Hume's In-Principle Argument

I believe there are at least two problems with Hume's in-principle argument: (1) It begs the question; and (2) It confuses evidence and probability.

1. A Question-Begging Argument. A number of thinkers have made the observation that Hume's argument begs the question.[50] Stephen Naylor Thomas defines a question-begging argument in the following way: "When reasoning, for one of its reasons or assumptions (whether explicit or suppressed), depends on a statement that is identical or equivalent to the drawn conclusion, then it is said to *'beg the question.'* Such an argument, which assumes the very claim it is trying to prove, is also called 'circular' or is said to 'argue in a circle.'"[51]

It is my contention that the degree to which Hume begs the question is contingent upon how one interprets his argument. For instance, if Hume defines nature as that which is by definition uniform, he clearly begs the question in favor of naturalism. This has been aptly pointed out by C.S. Lewis:

> Now of course we must agree with Hume that if there is absolutely "uniform experience" against miracles, if in other words they have never happened, why then they never have. Unfortunately, we know the experience against them to be uniform only if we know that all the reports of them are false. And we can know all the reports to be false only if we know already that miracles have never occurred. In fact, we are arguing in a circle.[52]

Is Lewis correct in his assessment of Hume's argument? Is Hume *really* arguing that nature is uniform? In answer to both questions: No. Given Hume's rejection of necessary connection,[53] and his reliance on an empiricist epistemology, it would stretch credibility to the limit to claim that Hume is arguing for the uniformity of nature. I think it is safe to say, however, that Hume is arguing that our *formulations* of natural law, if they are to be considered lawful appraisals of our perceptions, must be based on uniform *experience*, or they cease to be natural law. According to David Fate Norton's interpretation, this is the crux of Hume's argument:

If our experience of X's has been "firm and unalterable" or

28

"infallible," then we have, in Hume's scheme, a "proof" and are in a position to formulate a law of nature, or a summation of uniform experience. Correlatively, the moment we fail to have a proof, or perfect empirical support for any summation, we fail to have a law of nature.[54]

Hence, given that a law of nature must be what Hume calls a "proof," and proofs are by definition built on uniform and infallible experience, a violation of natural law would automatically disqualify the alleged law and would relegate it to the status of a probability. Norton continues:

> It is in this context that Hume grants (for the sake of argument, no doubt) that the evidence for a particular (alleged) miracle may be perfect of its kind. But even given this concession, he points out, there would be insufficient grounds for concluding that the event was a miracle, for there would be, contra this evidence, equally perfect evidence that the event has not taken place--the evidence of the uniform experience that is summarized by the (allegedly) violated law of nature. . . A miracle is a violation of the laws of nature; a law of nature is established by a firm and unalterable experience. The champion of miracles is arguing, however, that this experience is not firm and unalterable; at least, one exception is, he claims, known. From this exception it follows, Hume reminds us, that there is no violation of a law of nature because there is no law of nature, and hence, there is no miracle.[55]

What Norton is saying is simply this: a miracle is an event which is by definition a violation of natural law, but a violated law (because a natural law, by definition, is only such if based on uniform experience, i.e., a proof) is no longer a law. Hence, "the proof against a miracle, from the very nature of the fact, is as entire as any argument can possibly be established."[56]

Although this interpretation is much truer to the text than Lewis' interpretation, one could still argue that Hume begs the question in favor of naturalism (although the circle is certainly not as vicious as the one pointed out by Lewis). For the question can be asked: Why must one accept that a natural law cannot be a natural law if it has been violated? If the reply is that natural law cannot be otherwise, then the question has been begged, or Hume's argument against miracles is strictly tautological. Asserting that a natural law can only remain a natural law if it has not been violated is to assume that a violation can *count against* a natural law. In terms of Hume's own epistemology, this is entirely consistent, and for this reason, I believe that Norton is correct in his interpretation. It should be noted, however, that Hume

29

understood natural law in the sense that it was understood in his day: strictly determined and mechanistic. And it was against this version that he reacted, arguing that necessary connection could not be philosophically validated (hence, his appeal to unalterable *experience*). He thus rejected natural law as then understood, or at least he argued that one could not justify it philosophically.

However, I think that one can question Hume's view of natural law by showing that it is possible, and hence perfectly coherent, and in accord with both contemporary science and our experience of the world, to speak of a natural law and its violation. As Swinburne points out, in order to combat Hume's view of natural law "one must distinguish between a formula being a law [i.e., a law which can be violated and still remain a law] *and* a formula being (universally) true or being a law which holds without exception [i.e., Hume's view]."57

Prior to our examination of natural law, it is well worth pointing out George Mavrodes' observation that this interpretation of Hume's argument "need not be greatly disturbing to any religious person or any 'friend of miracles.'"58 After all, writes Mavrodes, the fact that these "violations" have undermined "natural law" does not mean they did not really occur. As he puts it:

> Nothing that the objector has said tends to show at all, or make it in any way probable, that Jesus did not turn water into wine, that he did not calm a storm with a word or raise Lazarus from the dead, and so on. Nor does it tend to show that these events did not have a profound religious significance. It does not even tend to show that these things, if they happened, were not miracles. At most (for better or worse) it tends to show that they are not *Humean* miracles.59

Returning to our examination of nature's laws, no doubt there is considerable debate among philosophers of science as to the precise technical meaning of the term "natural law." However, R.S. Walters writes that there is "agreement that a minimum necessary condition of a scientific statement proposed as lawlike is that it be a universal generalization."60 Swinburne defines what scientists generally mean by natural law when he writes that a natural law is that which describes "what happens in a *regular* and *predictable* way" (emphasis mine).61 Contrary to Hume's appeal to constant conjunction and proof (an unvaried constant conjunction), a natural law does *not* only describe what happens in the actual course of events, but explains the actual course of events in terms of hypothetical universal formulas (regular and predictable), e.g., If X has a certain mass, it will have a certain weight in earth's gravity. For if a natural law was merely descriptive of what regularly occurs and nothing more, the term "natural law" would be devoid of any cognitive content, similar to such assertions as "whatever will be will be." After all, scientists do reviews laws because of recurring anomalies, but rarely if ever on the basis of a *single* non-recurring anomaly which is nevertheless recognized as an anomaly (which obviously does not *count against* the law violated). Hence, natural laws must be cognitively significant assertions in which a true counter-factual is possible, whether it be a violation (a singular non-analogous anomaly) or a recurring anomaly. For this reason, if "what happens is entirely irregular and unpredictable [i.e., a violation], its occurrence is not something describable by natural laws." In other words, to "say that a certain such formula is a law is to say that in general its predictions are true and that any exceptions to its operations cannot be accounted for by another formula which could be taken as a law. . ."[62] Furthermore, as I pointed out in the second chapter, a violation of natural law is non-analogous; that is, it should not be confused with an anomaly which occurs regularly under like natural circumstances, which is usually a good indication that the law in question should be revised, replaced, or altered in some fashion so as to account for this anomaly under these particular circumstances.

Consider the following example. Suppose we have a natural law, L, which states that when a human being has been dead for 24 hours it is physically impossible for this corpse to become alive again. L is so intertwined with what has been well-established by years of anatomical, physiological, and biological study that no one doubts its status as a law; it is regular and predictable (i.e., "Given these circumstances, X, P will remain dead."). Every epitaph testifies to this chilling reality.

Suppose that on one Sunday afternoon a certain human being, H (let us say, a recognized holy person), who has been dead for more than 24 hours, gets up and walks out of the coroner's office. If this counter-instance to L, E, cannot be subsumed under either L or a more comprehensive law and it is a non-recurring anomaly, I do not see why it is incorrect to call E a legitimate violation of natural law without saying that L is no longer a natural law.

However, let us say that prior to his death H had drunk a yet undiscovered serum which has a natural chemical ability to restore life. Furthermore, let us say that the scientists studying this serum conclude that its chemical composition fits perfectly with what we already know about life, but yet takes us far beyond this knowledge. We are then forced to alter (although not completely change) some of our natural laws in light of this new discovery confirmed by repeatable experiment and observation (i.e., "If P drinks the serum prior to his death, P will resurrect within 36 hours of his death."): L will be replaced by a new law, L_2.

But if E cannot be subsumed under a more comprehensive law such as L_2, and we have good reason to believe that E would not occur again under similar circumstances (that is, it is a non-repeatable counter-instance), it is perfectly coherent to say that E is a violation of natural law

31

without saying that E counts against L. For E to be able to count against L it would have to be an anomaly repeatable under similar circumstances (such as in the case of the serum and L_2). "For these latter reasons it seems not unnatural to describe E as a non-repeatable counter-instance to a law of nature L..."[63]

In summary, to argue that natural law is based on "uniform experience," and that this epistemologically forbids one from asserting that a violation of natural law has occurred, is to beg the question in favor of naturalism (whether you take Lewis' or Norton's interpretation of Hume), for it is possible to be perfectly coherent in speaking of a violation of natural law without undermining the law's status as a law.

2. Proof, Probability, and Evidence. There are some scholars who acknowledge that it is possible to interpret Hume's in-principle argument to be "softer" than Norton interprets it to be.[64] This interpretation emphasizes Hume's rejection of miracles as a weighing of probabilities. Hume is arguing that the "proof" of the way nature generally functions (i.e., violations do not generally occur) outweighs the "proof" of the extremely rare occurrences of the miraculous. As Flew explains it: "But now, clearly, the evidence for the subsistence of such a strong order of Nature will have to be put on the side of the balance opposite to that containing the evidence for the occurrence of the exceptional overriding."[65] And for this reason, Flew asserts that Hume was *not* trying to establish "that miracles do not occur. . .; but that, whether or not they did or had, this is not something we can any of us ever be in a position positively to know."[66] In contrast to Norton, who views Hume's argument as demonstrating the logical inconsistency in holding to both the miraculous and natural law, Flew sees Hume's argument as a precursor to critical history.[67] Of course, it is possible to view these interpretations as two sides of the same coin. That is, Hume is showing both the logical (Norton's interpretation) and the testimonial (Flew's interpretation) problems of asserting that a violation of natural law has occurred. Since we have already shown that it is perfectly coherent to speak of violations of natural law, it is only the latter which remains as an obstacle to be hurdled.

Hume's weighing of probabilities in his miracles argument is entirely consistent with his epistemological foundation. All knowledge is derived from experience, and "a wise man. . . proportions his belief to the evidence."[68] As I noted earlier, for Hume, we are unable to know *the necessary connection* between any two events, but can only *believe* what we *customarily* infer from a constant conjunction. Consequently, when particular events continue to occur together, our *belief* that there is a causal connection present is given greater credibility. So in actuality what Hume means by "greater evidence" are events of greater repetition. This is why a miracle (which is a rare event) can never be believed for Hume: it is by definition evidentially weaker than the laws of nature it is being weighed against.

Now the problem with this argument is that Hume confuses evidence with probability. He asserts that we should always believe what is more probable, and whatever has occurred more often has greater probability in its favor, and hence greater evidence. One must weigh as evidence the antecedent improbability of a miraculous event occurring over against the particular evidence for the alleged event. Of course, based on this reasoning, it is never reasonable to believe that a miracle has occurred. Hume's assertion can be put this way:

(1) If E is a highly improbable event, no evidence is sufficient to warrant our belief that it has occurred.

This is certainly not a correct form of reasoning. Is it not the case that on the basis of sufficient evidence it is perfectly reasonable to believe that which is improbable has in fact occurred? A number of examples should help to demonstrate this.[69] Take for instance this well-documented case:

> . . . *Life* magazine once reported that all 15 people scheduled to attend a rehearsal of a church choir in Beatrice, Neb., were late for practice on March 1, 1950, and each had a different reason: a car wouldn't start, a radio program wasn't over, ironing wasn't finished, a conversation dragged on. It was fortunate that none arrived on schedule at 7:15 p.m.--the church was destroyed by an explosion at 7:25. The choir members wondered whether their mutual delays were an act of God. . . Weaver estimated there was a one-in-a-million chance that all 15 would be late the same evening.[70]

According to Hume's view of probability and evidence, it seems that a wise man should reject the reliable testimony and circumstantial evidence which has substantiated the fact of this occurrence, even though we know that no reasonable person would reject it.

It is highly improbable that my friend will be dealt a royal flush in a Las Vegas poker room, i.e., it is much more probable that he will be dealt a less promising hand (in fact, the probability of being dealt a royal flush is $0.15 \cdot 10^{-5}$).[71] But according to Hume's reasoning, if my friend is dealt a royal flush, which is a highly improbable occurrence, I should not believe the testimony of several reliable witnesses who claim to have seen the hand.

Finally, suppose a man, who had never murdered anyone in his life, is accused of murder and brought to trial. Five responsible and upstanding citizens, with no reason to lie about what they had witnessed, testify on the witness-stand that they had seen the accused commit an act of murder. However, the defense attorney, a follower of Hume, calls 925 people to the witness-stand to testify that they had known the accused for a good part of their lives and they had never seen him murder anybody. After this long parade of witnesses, the defense attorney argues: "Let us weigh the 'evidence' of all the people who have seen my client not murdering against the evidence of the five people who say that they had seen my client commit murder at one single moment. Since the 'evidence' ('proof') of non-murdering is greater than the evidence of murdering, and the intelligent person always sides with what has greater evidence, my client is *not* guilty." If the jury in this case is any jury at all, it would see through the clever charade this defense attorney is trying to pull; for they know that what is most probable (i.e., that which occurs most often, like non-murdering) can never be weighed as irrefutable "evidence" against the evidence of a rare occurrence (like murdering).

Now it may be the case that we have misunderstood Hume. After all, the above are examples of improbable, yet *natural*, events. Maybe he is saying that we should only disbelieve the testimonial and circumstantial evidence for violations of natural law, not just any improbable event. I think this is closer to what Hume is saying, for in one place Hume makes the interesting comment:

> I beg the limitations here made may be remarked, when I say, that a miracle can never be proved, so as to be the foundation of a system of religion. For I own, that otherwise, there may possibly be miracles, or violations of the usual course of nature, of such a kind as to admit the proof of human testimony; though, perhaps, it will be impossible to find any such in all the records of history. Thus, suppose, all authors, in all languages, agree, that, from the first of January 1600, there was a total darkness over the whole earth for eight days: suppose that the tradition of this extraordinary event is still strong and lively among the people: that all travellers, who return from foreign countries, bring us accounts of the same tradition, without the least variation or contradiction: it is evident, that our present philosophers, instead of doubting the fact, ought to receive it as certain, and ought to search for the causes whence it might be derived. The decay, corruption, and dissolution of nature, is an event rendered probable by so many analogies, that any phenomenon, which seems to have a tendency toward catastrophe, comes within the reach of human testimony, if that testimony be very extensive and uniform.[72]

Apparently Hume is saying that one can know that an improbable event has occurred, but that there is no reason to suppose that it does not have a natural explanation. Although he calls the above event a "miracle," it seems that Hume is using it in a different way than he did earlier in the text (i.e., in the sense of a bizarre or apparently law-violating event). This seems clear enough when Hume presents another example in which Queen Elizabeth dies (and the witnesses of her death are many and above reproach) and returns to claim her throne a month after her successor assumes it (and the same witnesses of her death are sure that it is the same Queen who has returned to her throne). Despite this apparently strong evidence for the Queen's resurrection, Hume declares that "I would still reply, that the knavery and folly of men are such common phenomena, that I should rather believe the most extraordinary events to arise from their occurrence, than admit of so signal a violation of the laws of nature."[73] Hume goes on to make two important points. First, even if the above event is ascribed to God, it does not make it any more probable, since we know only of God's attributes and actions in what we observe in the usual course of nature (i.e., nature is uniform). And from this Hume's second point follows: since in the usual course of nature it is more likely that a person not tell the truth about a religious miracle than the laws of nature be violated, it is more probable that the miracle did not occur.[74] The problems that lurk behind both these points--whether one can ascribe a divine source to a miraculous event, and whether religious people tend to exaggerate--will be discussed in the next two chapters.

However, let us first confront the claim that is implied in what Hume asserts in the employment of the above two stories. It seems that Hume is saying that if apparent violations of natural law occur, they either have a natural cause (and hence, they would not be *real* violations of natural law) or they did not really occur as the witnesses have described it. Hume's assertion can now be put this way:

(2) If E is a *real* violation of natural law, no evidence is sufficient to warrant our belief that it has occurred.

But since we have already seen that it is possible to be perfectly coherent in speaking of a violation of natural law, which is an improbable event, and sufficient testimony and evidence can make it reasonable to believe that an improbable event has occurred, to say that no testimony or evidence is sufficient to warrant our belief that a violation of natural law has occurred is to beg the question in favor of naturalism.

For the only way that Hume could rightfully argue that no evidence is sufficient to warrant our belief that a violation of natural law has occurred is if violations of natural law are maximally improbable. However, one can only know that violations are maximally improbable if one already *knows* that they could or have never occurred. But as Alvin Plantinga points out, ". . . why should a theist think that such a proposition [i.e., *E has occurred and E is a violation of a law of nature*] is maximally improbable? (Indeed, why should anyone think so? We aren't given *a priori* that nature is seldom interfered with.) Even if a theist thinks of miracles as a violation of laws of nature. . . she needn't think it improbable *in excelsis* that a miracle occur; so why couldn't she perfectly sensibly believe, on the basis of sufficient testimony, that some particular miraculous event has occurred?"[75] Therefore, the defender of Hume's argument cannot say that violations of natural law are maximally improbable unless he begs the question.

This is not to say that a wise person should not be skeptical of the testimony of an individual who claims to have witnessed a violation of natural law (or any highly improbable event for that matter). However, as J.C.A. Gaskin has pointed out: "There is an uncomfortable sense that by means of it [Hume's argument] one may well justify disbelieving reports of things which did in fact happen--like your disbelief in my report of seeing water turned into wine if my report had also been vouched by numerous other good and impartial witnesses."[76] He goes on to write:

> While it is certainly true that when something altogether extraordinary is reported, the wise man will require more evidence than usual and will check and re-check the evidence very carefully, nevertheless at some stage in his accumulation of respectable evidence the wise man would be in danger of becoming dogmatic and obscurantist if he did *not* believe the evidence.[77]

For example, suppose that someone tells you that he has just seen his father, who has been dead for the past two days, alive and walking the streets of New York City. You would be perfectly reasonable if you thought like Hume: "When someone tells me, that he saw a dead man restored to life, I immediately consider with myself, whether this person should either deceive or be deceived, or that the fact, which he relates should really have happened."[78] That is, it is more probable that deception is involved than that the testimony is accurate. After all, you would have no problem believing the testimony if this man's father had never died. This is because your expectations and judgments hinge on your previous experience: dead men do not come back to life. However, let us say that there are a number of reliable witnesses who corroborate this testimony. Furthermore, the mortuary, which had embalmed the body, reports that it is missing, and police confirm that the fingerprints of the living man (which they found on a glass he had touched) correspond perfectly to the fingerprints of the dead man. Moreover, the man in question was very religious and had prayed prior to his death asking God to resurrect him in order to demonstrate to his atheistic relatives the truth of his religious convictions.

In light of this example, it becomes apparent that Hume's weighing of probabilities is highly artificial, not to mention woefully

36

inadequate. In this case it is not a weighing of *a* probability, L (a law of nature), against *a* probability, T (a testimony claiming to have witnessed a violation of L), but a weighing of L against what Cardinal Newman called a "convergence of independent probabilities,"[79] T, T_1, T_2, . . . T_N (i.e., diverse and reliable testimonies, fingerprints, circumstantial evidence such as the missing embalmed body and his prayer to God, etc.).

As some have pointed out, just as our formulations of natural law are based on certain regularities, our standards of evaluating testimony and evidence are also based on certain regularities (e.g., "Witnesses in such-and-such a situation are more apt to tell the truth.").[80] Because these standards do not have the same individual probative strength as a natural law, a single piece, or even several pieces, of testimonial evidence in most cases is insufficient to warrant our belief that a violation of natural law has occurred (although a single testimony is usually sufficient to warrant belief in most everyday situations, such as "Honey, get the checkbook, the paper boy is here"). However, if the testimonial evidence is multiplied and reinforced by circumstantial considerations (as in the above example), and the explanation of the event as a violation connects the data in a simple and coherent fashion (just as we expect a natural law to do),[81] and a denial of the event's occurrence becomes an *ad hoc* naturalism-of-the-gaps,[82] I do not see why it would not be entirely reasonable to believe that this event has occurred (based on a convergence of independent probabilities). I believe that this approach retains a healthy Humean skepticism by taking into consideration the improbability of a miraculous event, but I also believe that it resists a dogmatic skepticism by taking seriously the possibility that one may have evidence for a miracle.

This in no way denies Hume's point that we make our judgments on the basis of uniformity, regularity, and probability. Rather, the point is being made that Hume incorrectly assumed that because we *base* our knowledge of the past on regularities (constant conjunction) the *object* of our knowledge must therefore be a regular event and not one that is either singular or highly improbable Therefore, since we base both evidential and natural law judgments on regularities, it is certainly possible that we can have sufficient evidence to believe that an event highly improbable in terms of natural law has occurred. For if the question of a miracle's occurrence is relegated exclusively to whether the event is improbable in terms of our general experience, then we would be forced to the absurd conclusion that we can never know that an improbable event has occurred; but we do in fact know that some improbable events have occurred. Hence, the question of the event's probability of having occurred must be answered in terms of the evidence for its occurrence on this single occasion, not exclusively on its antecedent improbability. That is why it is entirely reasonable to believe that the above examples of improbable events have in fact occurred: evidential considerations, based on certain regularities, were able to "outweigh" the antecedent improbability of the event occurring.[83]

As to what standards or criteria would be employed in judging the adequacy of the evidence of any alleged violation of natural law which is a miracle, we will put aside until chapter 7 of this book. For the time being, however, it is only necessary that we justify the possibility that sufficient testimony and evidence can warrant our belief that a violation of natural law has occurred. I believe that this task has been accomplished. In summary, Hume has failed to realize that the wise and intelligent person bases his or her convictions on *evidence*, not on Humean "probability". That is, an event's occurrence may be very improbable in terms of past experience and observation, but current observation and testimony may lead one to believe that the evidence for the event is good. In this way, Hume confuses evidence with probability.

[1]David Hume, *An Enquiry Concerning Human Understanding*, 3rd edition, text revised and notes P.H. Nidditch, intro. and analytic index L.A. Selby-Bigge (Oxford: Clarendon, 1975; reprinted 1777 edition). It should be noted that John Passmore writes that the tenth section of the *Enquiry*, "Of Miracles," "was originally meant to form part of the *Treatise* [*on Human Nature*, 1739-1740]; and without it the *Treatise* is incomplete." (John Passmore, *Hume's Intentions*, rev. ed. [New York: Basic Books, 1952], p. 32) Concerning this point, Hume writes in a letter to Henry Home: "Having a frankt letter, I was resolved to make use of it; and accordingly inclose some *Reasonings Concerning Miracles*, which I once thought of publishing with the rest, but which I am afraid will give too much offence, even as the world is disposed at present." (J.Y.T. Greig, ed., *The Letters of David Hume*, 2 vols. [Oxford: Clarendon, 1932], 1:24). See also, John O. Nelson, "The Burial and Resurrection of Hume's Essay 'Of Miracles'," *Hume Studies*, 12 (April 1986): 57-76.

[2]Francis Bacon, *The New Organon* (New York: Bobbs-Merrill, 1960)

[3]John Locke, *An Essay Concerning Human Understanding*, ed. P.H. Nidditch (Oxford: Clarendon, 1975). It is interesting to note that Locke, in contrast to Hume, defended the historicity of the miraculous. See John Locke, *The Reasonableness of Christianity* with *A Discourse on Miracles* and part of *A Third Letter Concerning Toleration*, ed. I.T. Ramsey (Stanford, CA: Stanford University Press, 1958)

[4]George Berkeley, *A Treatise Concerning the Principles of Human Knowledge* (LaSalle, IL: Open Court, 1946)

[5]Hume, *Enquiry*, p. 18.

[6]David Hume, *A Treatise of Human Nature*, 2nd edition, text revised and notes P.H. Nidditch, analytic index L.A. Selby-Bigge (Oxford: Clarendon, 1978; reproduced 1739-40 edition), pp. 2-7.

[7]*Ibid.*, p. 2.

[8]For example, Hume writes, "There is, however, one contradictory phenomenon, which may prove, that it is not absolutely impossible for ideas to arise, independent of their correspondent impressions. I believe it will readily be allowed, that the several distinct ideas of colour, which enter by the eye, or those of sound, which are conveyed by the ear, are really different from each other; though, at the same time resembling. Now if this be true of different colours, it must be no less so of the different shades of the same colour; and each shade produces a

distinct idea, independent of the rest. For if this should be denied, it is possible, by the continual gradation of shades, to run a colour insensibly into what is most remote from it; and if you will not allow any of the means to be different, you cannot, without absurdity, deny the extremes to be the same. Suppose, therefore, a person to have enjoyed his sight for thirty years, and to have become perfectly acquainted with colours of all kinds, except one particular shade of blue, for instance, which it never has been his fortune to meet with. Let all the different shades of that colour, except that single one, be placed before him, descending gradually from the deepest to the lightest; it is plain, that he will perceive a blank, where that shade is wanting, and will be sensible, that there is a greater distance in that place between the contiguous colours than in any other. Now I ask, whether it be possible for him, from his own imagination, to supply this deficiency, and raise up to himself the idea of that particular shade, though it had never been conveyed to him by the senses? I believe there are few but will be of opinion that he can: And this may serve as a proof, that the simple ideas are not always, in every instance, derived from the correspondent impressions; though this instance is so singular, that it is scarcely worth our observing, and does not merit that for it alone we should alter our general maxim." (Hume, *Enquiry*, pp. 20-21)

9Hume, *Enquiry*, p. 19, and Hume, *Treatise*, p. 3.

10Hume, *Enquiry*, p. 25.

11*Ibid.*, pp. 25-26.

12*Ibid.*, p. 25.

13*Ibid.*, p. 165. In contemporary philosophy, certain analytic philosophers make a similar distinction. They call matters of fact, *synthetic statements*, and they call relations of ideas, *analytic statements*.

14Hume, *Enquiry*, p. 26

15*Ibid.*, p. 43.

16*Ibid.* Hume's view of causality included more than mere constant conjunction and was more complicated than just arising from "custom alone." However, since Hume's more fully elaborated presentation of his view is found in the *Treatise*, and it is our said purpose to briefly summarize the epistemological context in which "Of Miracles" appears (that is, the *Enquiry*), I refer the reader to Hume's *Treatise*, parts I, II, and III.

[17]However, when it comes to his criticism of the argument from design, Hume acknowledges this point: "When, therefore, we find, that any work has proceeded from the skill and industry of man; as we are otherwise acquainted with the nature of the animal, we can draw a hundred inferences concerning what may be expected from him; and these inferences will all be founded in experience and observation. But did we know man only from the single work or production which we examine, it were impossible for us to argue in this manner; because our knowledge of all the qualities, which we ascribe to him, being in that case derived from the production, it is impossible they could point to anything farther, or be the foundation of any new inference." (*Ibid.*, p. 144)

[18]Hume, *Enquiry*, p. 30.

[19]*Ibid.*, p. 58-59.

[20]*Ibid.*, p. 56. In the *Treatise* (p. 124), Hume defines *proof* and *probability* in the following way: "By knowledge, I mean the assurance arising from the comparison of ideas. By *proofs*, those arguments, which are deriv'd from the relation of cause and effect, and which are entirely free from doubt and uncertainty. By *probability*, that evidence, which is still attended with uncertainty. 'Tis this last species of reasoning, I proceed to examine."

[21]Hume, *Enquiry*, pp. 57-58. Although Hume makes a distinction between *the probability of chances* and *the probability of causes* (*Enquiry*, pp. 56-59; and *Treatise*, pp. 124-142), it is only the latter (the one put forth in the text of this dissertation) which has a bearing on his miracles argument. Differing in depth and emphasis, the following works are suggested readings on Hume and probability: Antony Flew, *David Hume: Philosopher of Moral Science* (New York: Basil Blackwell, 1986), pp. 56-60, 123-126; Norman Kemp Smith, *The Philosophy of David Hume* (London: Macmillan, 1941), pp. 414-430; and D.C. Stove, *Probability and Hume's Inductive Skepticism* (Oxford: Clarendon, 1973).

[22]John V. Price, *David Hume* (New York: Twayne Publishers, 1968), pp. 42, 43.

[23]Colin Brown, *Miracles and the Critical Mind* (Grand Rapids, Mich.: Eerdmans, 1984), p. 79.

[24]Antony Flew, *Hume's Philosophy of Belief* (London: Routledge & Kegan Paul, 1961), p. 171.

[25]Benedict De Spinoza, *Tractatus Theologico-Politicus*, in *The Chief Works of Benedict de Spinoza*, trans. R.H.M. Elwes, 2 vols. (London: George Bell

and Sons, 1883), 1:83ff.

[26]See "The Age of Deism," chapter 3 of Brown, *Miracles*, pp. 47-77. In his *Dictionary of the English Language* (1755), Dr. Samuel Johnson defined a "deist" as "a man who follows no particular religion, but only acknowledges the existence of God, without any other article of faith." (As quoted in Brown, *Miracles*, p. 47). For an excellent presentation and critique of deism, see Norman L. Geisler and William D. Watkins, *Worlds Apart: A Handbook on World Views*, 2nd ed. (Grand Rapids, Baker Book House, 1989), pp. 147-185.

[27]Conyers Middleton, *A Free Inquiry into the Miraculous Powers Which are Supposed to have Subsisted in the Christian Church, from the Earliest Ages through Several Successive Centuries, To which is Added a Letter from Rome, Shewing Exact Conformity between Popery and Paganism: or the Religion of the Present Romans, Derived from from that of their Heathen Ancestors* (London: Sherwood and Co., 1825)

[28]Brown, *Miracles*, p. 79. David Fate Norton writes that "although Hume mildly bemoans (in his *My Own Life*) the fact that Conyers Middleton's *Free Enquiry into the Miraculous Powers. . .* upstaged his own *Enquiry*, it is nonetheless true that the sceptical religious tendency of the latter work was very soon noted and responded to." (David Fate Norton, *David Hume: Common-Sense Moralist, Sceptical Metaphysician* [Princeton, NJ: Princeton University Press, 1982], p. 295). See also, Ernest Campbell Mossner, *The Life of David Hume* (Oxford: Clarendon, 1954), p. 223.

[29]Hume, *Treatise*, p. 241ff. Richard H. Popkin points out how Spinoza and Hume differ in their rejection of miracles: "Spinoza constructed a metaphysical world in which a Providential God was impossible. . . [M]iracles were not implausible; they were impossible. . . Instead of rejecting religious history on metaphysical grounds, Hume tried to do it empirically, in part, by arguing that it was empirically unlikely that religious events occurred and, in part, by arguing that our empirical knowledge of the Deity excluded any prophetic information. The world that was left to know was not Spinoza's one substance, but just the course of events." (Richard H. Popkin, "Hume: Historical Versus Prophetic Historian," in *David Hume: Many-Sided Genius*, ed. Kenneth R. Merrill and Robert W. Shahan [Norman, OK: University of Oklahoma Press, 1976], p. 90).

[30]See Hume, *Enquiry*, sections XI and XII, pp. 132-165; and David Hume, *Dialogues Concerning Natural Religion*, ed. and intro. Norman Kemp Smith (New York: Bobbs-Merrill, 1947; 1779 edition).

[31]William Lane Craig, "Colin Brown, *Miracles and the Critical Mind*: A

Review Article," *Journal of the Evangelical Theological Society*, 27 (December 1984): 476.

[32]Hume, *Enquiry*, pp. 114-116.

[33]Tillotson (1630-1694), a Presbyterian theologian and Archbishop of Canterbury (1691-1694), argued in both his *Rule of Faith* (1676) and *A Discourse Against Transubstantiation* (1684) that it is not possible to establish transubstantiation as part of Christian doctrine.

[34]Hume, *Enquiry*, p. 109.

[35]Tillotson, *A Discourse Against Transubstantiation*, Vol. II, p. 448, as quoted in Flew, *Hume's Philosophy of Belief*, p. 172. For an extended discussion of Tillotson's argument and how Hume applies it, see Dennis M. Ahern, "Hume on the Evidential Impossibility of Miracles," in *Studies in Epistemology*, *APQ* Monograph No. 9, ed. Nicholas Rescher (Oxford: Basil Blackwell, 1975), pp. 14-30. Ahern writes in detail of the possible ways one can interpret Hume's use of Tillotson, and concludes that a similar interpretation to mine possesses independent plausibility and is a viable interpretation of Hume's argument. Although the interpretation of Tillotson's argument and how it relates to Hume's argument is a worthy topic, for both the sake of brevity and the importance of dealing exclusively with the specific content of Hume's argument, I refer the reader to Ahern's excellent work.

[36]Hume, *Enquiry*, p. 110.

[37]*Ibid.*, pp. 110-111.

[38]*Ibid.*, p. 112.

[39]*Ibid.*

[40]*Ibid.*, p. 113.

[41]*Ibid.*

[42]*Ibid.*

[43]*Ibid.*, p. 114. Concerning Hume's use of the term "unalterable," J.C.A. Gaskin's comments are worth noting: "Even here there is an incipient mistake. The word 'unalterable,' although justifiable on some account of the laws of nature, is not justifiable on Hume's. What he should have written is something like 'unvaried'." (J.C.A. Gaskin, *Hume's Philosophy of Religion* [London: Macmillan, 1978], p. 122).

[44]*Ibid.*, p. 115.

[45]This is an example used by Richard Swinburne, *The Concept of Miracle* (New York: Macmillan, 1970), p. 14.

[46]Hume, *Enquiry*, pp. 115-116.

[47]*Ibid.*, p. 116.

[48]*Ibid.*

[49]*Ibid.*, p. 110.

[50]For example, Craig, *Apologetics*, pp. 121-122; Norman L. Geisler, *Miracles and Modern Thought* (Grand Rapids, Mich.: Zondervan, 1982), pp. 27-30; Habermas, "Skepticism: Hume," pp. 42-44; C.S. Lewis, *Miracles* (Great Britain: Fontana, 1947), pp. 104-107; and John Warwick Montgomery, *Principalities and Powers* (Minneapolis: Bethany House, 1973), pp. 43-46.
　　James Noxon writes: "If Hume really intended his critique 'Of Miracles' to 'establish it as a maxim, that no human testimony can have such a force as to prove a miracle, and make it a foundation for any such system of religion'. . ., his argument is a question-begging failure." (James Noxon, "Hume's Concern With Religion," in *David Hume: Many-Sided Genius*, p. 77).

[51]Stephen Naylor Thomas, *Practical Reasoning in Natural Language*, 3rd ed. (Englewood Cliffs, NJ: Prentice-Hall, 1986), p. 370.

[52]Lewis, *Miracles*, p. 106.

[53]See Robert J. Roth, S.J., "Did Peirce Answer Hume On Necessary Connection?" *Review of Metaphysics*, 38 (June 1985): 867-880.

[54]Norton, *David Hume*, p. 298.

[55]*Ibid.*, p. 299.

[56]Hume, *Enquiry*, p. 114.

[57]Swinburne, *Concept*, p. 28.

[58]George Mavrodes, "Miracles and the Laws of Nature," *Faith and Philosophy*, 2 (October 1985): 337.

[59]*Ibid.*

[60]R.S. Walters, "Laws of Science and Lawlike Statements," in *Encyclopedia*

of Philosophy, vol. 4, ed. Paul Edwards (New York: Macmillan & The Free Press, 1967), pp. 410-411. See John Hospers, "Law," in *Introductory Readings in the Philosophy of Science*, eds. E.D. Klemke, Robert Hollinger, and A. David Kline (Buffalo, NY: Prometheus Books, 1980), pp. 104-111; Charles E. Hummell, *The Galileo Connection* (Downers Grove, IL: Inter-Varsity Press, 1986), pp. 180-188; and Ernest Nagel, *The Structure of Science* (New York: Harcourt, Brace, 1961), pp. 75-78.

61Swinburne, *Concept*, p. 26. This view of scientific law as regular and predictable is echoed by Hummell, Walters, and Patrick Nowell-Smith. Hummell writes: "Since laws are based directly on experimental data, they can be tested at any time. They not only describe present natural phenomena but also precisely predict future results for a given set of conditions. Thus they also provide the basis for technology, the use of science for practical purposes." (Hummell, *Galileo*, p. 184. Walters asserts: "Suppose it is a law, *s*, that sodium burns when exposed to air. This law. . . can explain why a given piece of sodium burns when exposed to air and can be used to predict that all, scientists do revise laws because of recurring anomalies, a given piece of sodium will burn when exposed to air." (Walters, "Laws," p. 412). Patrick Nowell-Smith, whose article is written in opposition to belief in miracles, writes that "a scientific explanation is an hypothesis from which predictions can be made, which can afterwards be verified. It is the essence of such an hypothesis--a 'law' is but a well-confirmed hypothesis--that it should be capable of such predictive expansion." (Patrick Nowell-Smith, "Miracles," in *New Essays in Philosophical Theology*, eds. Antony Flew and Alasdair MacIntyre [New York: Macmillan, 1955], pp. 249-250).

62Swinburne, *Concept*, pp. 26, 27-28.

63*Ibid.*, p. 27.

64For example, see Craig, *Apologetics*, pp. 121-122; Flew, *David Hume: Philosopher of Moral Science*, p. 81f.; Geisler, *Miracles*, pp. 28-34; R.F. Holland, "The Miraculous," in *Logical Analysis and Contemporary Theism*, ed. John Donnelly (New York: Fordham University Press, 1972), pp. 226-235; and Noxon, "Hume's Concern," pp. 73-82.

65Flew, *Hume: Philosopher of Moral Science*, p. 81.

66*Ibid.*, p. 80.

67Referring to how Hume's argument affects the defender of miracles, Norton writes: "His conceptions are, to say the least, incompatible, and thus to argue that there are both uniformities and miracles is inconsistent." (Norton, *David Hume*, p. 299). Flew writes that Hume's work on miracles shows "what Hume never manages outright to say, that the critical historian, in approaching the detritus of the past, has to assume whatever he knows, or thinks that he knows, about what is probable or improbable, possible or impossible. For it is only upon these always fallible and corrigible assumptions that he becomes able to interpret any of that detritus as historical evidence at all; much less to erect upon it his account of what did and did not actually happen." (Flew, *David Hume: Philosopher of Moral Science*, p. 84).

This is not to say that Flew does not see the epistemological problem inherent in the concept of miracle as it relates to natural law, for he in fact has written on this problem elsewhere. However, in contrast to Norton, Flew denies that Hume himself specifically argues in this way: "all this argumentation, although (in spirit at least) thoroughly Humean, has little to do with the line of argumentation which Hume chose to develop in the section 'Of Miracles'." (Antony Flew, "Miracles," in *Encyclopedia of Philosophy*, vol. 5, p. 349).

[68]Hume, *Enquiry*, p. 110.

[69]As I mentioned in note 21, Hume writes of two types of probability, probability of chances and probability of causes. The former is similar to what probability theorists call the *a priori* theory of probability, and the latter is similar to what they call the relative-frequency theory of probability. An example of how both theories work can be seen in the odds of a flipped coin landing on heads. According to the *a priori* theory, prior to any flip, the odds are 1/2 that the coin will land on heads. In contrast, the relative-frequency theory measures the frequency of an event having occurred, and then a probability is calculated in light of this frequency. According to this theory, a coin which has landed on heads six times out of ten flips has a probability of 3/5, or .600. Irving Copi uses the following example to explain the relative-frequency view: ". . .the probability of a twenty-five-year old woman surviving her twenty-sixth birthday is .971 . . . Of 1,000 twenty-five-year-old women, if 971 exhibit the attribute of surviving at least one additional year, the number .971 is assigned as the probability coefficient for the occurrence of this attribute in any such class." (Irving M. Copi, *Introduction to Logic*, 5th Edition [New York: Macmillan, 1978], pp. 510, 513).

As I mentioned earlier, the probability of causes, which roughly corresponds to the relative-frequency theory of probability, is the view I believe Hume speaks of in his miracles argument. However, for the sake of covering all bases, in the text I will use examples of improbable events of both sorts (*a priori* and relative-frequency), which reasonable people should believe on the basis of sufficient evidence.

[70]Richard Blodgett, "Our Wild, Weird World of Coincidence," in *Reader's Digest*, 131 (September 1987): 127.

[71]Richard A. Epstein, *The Theory of Gambling and Statistical Logic* (New York: Academic Press, 1967), p. 222.

[72]Hume, *Enquiry*, pp. 127-128

[73]*Ibid.*, p. 128.

[74]*Ibid.*, p. 129.

[75]Alvin Plantinga, "Is Theism Really a Miracle?" *Faith and Philosophy*, 3 (April 1986): 113. Another interesting response to Hume's argument from probability along the same lines is Roy A. Sorensen's observation that "one cannot establish this kind of scepticism merely by showing that the correctness of any report of a miracle is improbable. One must show that the low probabilities of the individual testimonies do not add up in such a way as to make probable 'There is at least one miracle'." He concludes, "Hume's argument does not rule out the possibility that one accepts case by case scepticism and yet one knows through testimony that at least one miracle took place." (Roy A. Sorenson, "Hume's Scepticism Concerning Reports of Miracles," *Analysis*, 43 [January 1983]: 60).
    My argument for the possibility of miracles below, based on the convergence of independent probabilities, could be viewed as an extrapolation of Sorenson's observation.

[76]Gaskin, *Hume's Philosophy of Religion*, p. 115.

[77]*Ibid.*

[78]Hume, *Enquiry*, p. 116.

[79]As cited in John Warwick Montgomery, "Science, Theology, and the Miraculous," in his *Faith Founded on Fact* (New York: Thomas Nelson, 1978), p. 55.

[80]See Swinburne, *Concept*, pp. 41-48. Montgomery explains that legal reasoning is an example of evidential criteria based on certain regularities: "The lawyer endeavors to reduce societal conflicts by arbitrating conflicting truth-claims. Inherent to the practice of the law is an effort to resolve conflicts over legal responsibilities, and such conflicts invariably turn on questions of fact. To establish a 'cause of action' the plaintiff's complaint must allege a legal right which the defendant was duty-bound to recognize, and which he violated; at the trial evidentiary facts must be marshaled in support of the plaintiff's allegations, and the defendant will need to provide factual evidence in his behalf to counter the plaintiff's prima facie case against him. To this end, legal science, as an outgrowth of millennia of court decisions,

developed meticulous criteria for distinguishing factual truth from error." (John Warwick Montgomery, *The Law Above the Law* [Minneapolis: Dimension Books, 1975], p. 86)

[81]Swinburne writes: "So then a claim that a formula L is a law of nature and a claim that testimony or trace of a certain type is reliable are established basically the same way--by showing that certain formulae connect observed data in a simple coherent way." (Swinburne, *Concept*, p. 43).

That simplicity and coherence are values which the scientist seeks in formulating any law or theory is defended by not a few philosophers of science. For example, see W.H. Newton-Smith, *The Rationality of Science* (London: Routledge & Kegan Paul, 1981), pp. 226-232; Karl R. Popper, "Truth, Rationality, and the Growth of Knowledge," in his *Conjectures and Refutations* (New York: Harper & Row, 1963), pp. 240-241; and Hilary Putnam, *Reason, Truth, and History* (New York: Cambridge University Press, 1981), p. 35.

[82]A fine example of naturalism-of-the-gaps is Hume's defense of maintaining naturalism in his fictional account of Queen Elizabeth's resurrection. See Hume, *Enquiry*, p. 128.

[83]I am not the first to employ Hume's own view of probability against him. John King-Farlow cites a work of the little known philosopher and scientist Charles Babbage, *Ninth Bridgewater Treatise* (first published, 1837), in which Babbage employs numerical probability to quantify the probability of a miraculous resurrection and the probability of witnesses to give accurate testimony of such an occurrence. He concludes that it is sometimes reasonable to believe that a miracle has occurred. Although I do not agree entirely with his approach, I believe Babbage was on the right track. See John King-Farlow, "Historical Insights on Miracles: Babbage, Hume, Aquinas," *International Journal for Philosophy of Religion*, 13 (1982): 209-218.

CHAPTER FOUR

HUME'S ARGUMENT, PART 2:
THE HISTORICAL-CRITERIA ARGUMENT

In part I of his chapter on miracles, Hume argues that *even if* there is strong evidence for a miraculous event, the intelligent person should reject it. As we saw in our critique, this part of Hume's argument contains several flaws. J.C.A. Gaskin believes that Hume began part II with "what is clearly a premeditated retraction. . .as if sensing that his argument [part I] could be unconvincing when brought to bear upon evidence which in itself amounted to a full proof."[1] That is why Hume argues in part II that *in fact* "there never was a miraculous event established on so full an evidence."[2] He comes to this conclusion by applying historical criteria consisting of four elements. Hume writes that there is insufficient evidence for asserting that an alleged miracle constitutes a proof, because no alleged miracle has been able to overcome the following problems: (1) There is lacking a sufficient amount of good witnesses; (2) Human nature tends to exaggerate; (3) Miraculous stories originate among the uneducated and ignorant; and (4) Miracle stories of conflicting religious systems cancel each other. Our critical analysis will scrutinize the soundness and logical structure of these criteria.

THERE IS LACKING A SUFFICIENT AMOUNT OF GOOD WITNESSES

Hume makes the assertion that "in all history" there has never been "any miracle attested by a sufficient number of men, of such unquestioned good-sense, education, and learning, as to secure us against all delusion in themselves." In other words, there has never been a miracle that has been witnessed by anyone "of such undoubted integrity, as to place them beyond all suspicion of any design to deceive others; of such credit and reputation in the eyes of mankind as to have a great deal to lose in case their being detected in any falsehood." He also claims that the witnesses of alleged miracles have never made their claims about a miracle which was "performed in such a public manner, in so celebrated a part of the world, as to render the detection unavoidable."[3]

In many respects this is certainly not an entirely unreasonable criterion put forth by Hume. One would expect when examining any alleged eyewitness testimony that the eyewitnesses be of a sufficient number and character. However, Hume's criterion demands much more than this. As Colin Brown has accurately observed:

. . . the qualifications he demands of such witnesses are such as would preclude the testimony of anyone without a Western university education, who lived outside a major cultural center in Western Europe prior the sixteenth century, and who was not a public figure.[4]

One might be tempted to believe that Hume has put forth a criterion, not so much to describe what he thought sufficient and good witnesses might be, but rather with the prejudicial disposition of purposely dispensing with any testimony having its origin in the ancient world. But the fact of the matter is that "the calendar" and the amount of time spent in a classroom in a major Western university have never been considered *de facto* earmarks of moral and personal integrity. As one of my former professors said a number of years ago, "If one succeeds in educating a liar, one only succeeds in making him a better liar." Intellectual acumen and philosophical sophistication are not attributes that predispose one to impeccable ethical conduct.

Furthermore, although this is not a book in historical apologetics, it is well worth mentioning that some of the latest scholarship lends support to the contention that the crowning miracle of Christian theism, the Resurrection of Jesus, seems to fulfill Hume's first criterion.[5] Considering that it is acknowledged that Hume's argument is implicitly directed at the miracles of Christianity[6] (and in particular, Thomas Sherlock's defense of the Resurrection of Jesus, *The Tryal of the Witnesses*[7]), the above point, and subsequent observations about Hume's argument and the Christian miracles, should not be overlooked.

However, it should be pointed out that when Hume finally does apply his criterion to an alleged miracle which appears to fulfill it, his standards no longer seem attainable. Take for example the case of the Jansenist miracles:

> There surely never was a greater number of miracles ascribed to one person, than those, which were lately said to have been wrought in France upon the Tomb of Abbe' Paris, the famous Jansenist, with whose sanctity the people were so long deluded. The curing of the sick, giving hearing to the deaf, and sight to the blind, were every where talked of as the usual effects of the holy sepulchre. But what is more extraordinary; many of the miracles were immediately proved upon the spot, before judges of unquestioned integrity, attested by witnesses of credit and distinction, in a learned age, and on the most eminent theatre that is now in the world. Nor is this all: a relation of them was published and dispersed every where; nor were the *Jesuits*, though a learned body, supported by the civil magistrate, and determined enemies to those opinions, in whose favour the miracles were said to have been wrought, ever able

> distinctly to refute or detect them. Where shall we find such a number of circumstances, agreeing to the corroboration of one fact? And what have we to oppose to such a cloud of witnesses, but the absolute impossibility or miraculous nature of the events, which they relate? And this surely, in the eyes of all reasonable people, will alone be regarded as a sufficient refutation.[8]

Swinburne writes, "Here the credibility of the witnesses in terms of their number, integrity and education is dismissed, not as inadequate, but as irrelevant."[9] But as we have already pointed out in Chapter 2, the antecedent improbability of an event (which I take "absolute impossibility" to mean in this passage) can not rule out *a priori* that there can never be sufficient evidence to warrant our belief that it has occurred. To think otherwise is simply to beg the question in favor of naturalism, which is exactly what Hume does in his analysis of the Jansenist miracles. This criterion, although reasonable in its demand for sufficient eyewitness testimony (to which the believer in miracles will unhesitantly agree), is extremely naive in assuming that the modern world (the intellectual elites of Hume's 18th-century Western Europe) has a monopoly on moral integrity.

HUMAN NATURE TENDS TO EXAGGERATE

Hume asserts that "we observe in human nature a principle, which, if strictly examined, will be found to diminish extremely the assurance, which we might, from human testimony, have, in any kind of prodigy." This "principle" of human nature is exhibited in people's tendency to believe the incredible, and to exaggerate the content of certain events. Hume claims that because there is a "strong propensity of mankind to the extraordinary and the marvellous," we "ought reasonably to beget a suspicion against relations of this kind." Hume warns us that "if the spirit of religion join itself to the love of wonder, there is an end of common-sense; and human testimony, in these circumstances, loses all pretensions to authority." The believer may even know that the miracle-story is false, but according to Hume, this means nothing. The believer, writes Hume, will "persevere in it, for the sake of promoting so holy a cause."[10]

Few doubt the fact that some allegedly miraculous events are the product of human imagination and the desire to believe the wonderful,[11] but one cannot deduce from this that *all* alleged miracles did not take place. For to do so would be to commit the *fallacy of false analogy*. According to Vincent E. Barry and Douglas J. Soccio this fallacy "*is an argument that makes an erroneous comparison. Generally, we make erroneous comparisons by ignoring significant disanalogies between the things* compared."[12]

For example, let us say that an alleged miracle, M, has all the earmarks of the false miracles, F's, we have previously encountered, i.e., lack of good witnesses, lack of corroborating evidence, sufficient time for legend to accumulate, inability to discount naturalistic explanations, witnesses having a history of telling tall tales, etc. Hence we conclude that exaggeration and credulity were involved, and because M is analogous to F's, it is perfectly reasonable to disbelieve that M has occurred. However, if an alleged miracle, M_1, does not have any of the earmarks of any F's, there is no *prima facia* reason to discount the reality of M_1 on the basis of any analogy to like events (i.e., there is no positive analogy). After all, you cannot assume that all miracle-claims are involved in exaggeration unless you already know that miracles never occur. And the only way we can have good reason to believe that a particular miracle claim is a product of exaggeration, and hence did not take place, is if the *evidence* or the lack thereof tends to confirm this fact (that is, we know enough about a particular case, and cases analogous to it, to make this judgment). Therefore, to claim that exaggeration is always involved in miracle-claims without seeing whether in fact a positive analogy is actually present is to beg the question in favor of naturalism.

In addition, Brown has pointed out that Hume "is irresponsible to brand all religious people as naturally prone to disseminate untruth whether wittingly or unwittingly." He writes that Hume "fails to take into account the possibility that some people, including religious people, are by nature skeptics."[13] Swinburne has written that there are "some religious people who lean over backwards in their attempts to report their observations honestly."[14] In this regard, one immediately thinks of the Vatican's rigorous scrutiny of miracle-claims attributed to particular "saints". Therefore, we can not resolve the question of the validity of a particular miracle-claim by discounting all miracle-claims because some human beings exaggerate wonderful events. Rather, we should examine the *particular* people involved in the *particular* claim of an alleged miracle. "How many people are in each group, and in which group are the witnesses to any alleged miracle are matters for particular historical investigation."[15]

MIRACLES ORIGINATE AMONG THE UNEDUCATED AND THE IGNORANT

According to Hume, "it forms a strong presumption against all supernatural and miraculous relations, that they are observed chiefly to abound among ignorant and barbarous nations. . ." And if reasonably sophisticated moderns believe miracle-stories, it is usually because they "have received them from ignorant and barbarous ancestors, who transmitted them with that inviolable sanction and authority, which always attend received opinions." He explains that there is a great advantage in miracle stories originating among the ignorant in an obscure land. For "it has a much better chance of succeeding in remote countries, than if the first scene had been laid in a city renowned for arts and knowledge."[16]

There are at least three problems with this third criterion: (1) Hume does not adequately define what he means by an uneducated and ignorant people; (2) This criterion does not apply to the miracles of Christian theism; and (3) Hume commits the informal fallacy *argumentum ad hominem*. Concerning the first problem, Swinburne has correctly observed that Hume's third criterion "depends on what counts as an ignorant or barbarous nation."[17] However, in order for this criterion to be meaningful Hume cannot simply claim that an ignorant nation is "'one which is disposed to believe purported miracles.' For in that case his claim would be analytically true (true, that is, in virtue of the meaning of the terms used, as is 'all bachelors are unmarried')."[18] And hence it would be question-begging.

Moreover, it would not suffice for Hume to claim that he defines "ignorant," "uneducated," or "barbarous" as "not possessing modern scientific beliefs." For it is clear that "most nations except modern western nations would then by that definition be ignorant, and so most beliefs are likely to abound among the former nations simply because there are many more of them."[19]

Finally, if Hume means by ignorant those countries which lack any sort of science or literature, his case against miracles fails. "Many nations, for example in the Middle Ages, with a considerable literature and a solid, although not progressive, body of scientific knowledge, have abounded with reports of miracles."[20]

It is worth repeating that Hume dismissed the Jansenist miracles-- which occurred "in a learned age, and on the most eminent theatre that is now in the world"[21]--although they fulfilled this criterion. In light of this, it seems that Hume is not only unclear as to the meaning of an ignorant and uneducated people, his criterion appears incapable of actually being applied in counting for or against a particular miracle claim.

Concerning the second problem, the miracles of Christian theism did not arise out of an ignorant and uneducated nation. This has been adequately documented in note 8. And thirdly, Hume commits the informal fallacy *argumentum ad hominem*, an argument in which "we attack the person with whom we're contesting and not the person's argument."[22] Without disproving the veracity of a particular testimony to the miraculous, Hume attacks the person who is testifying: this person should not be believed because he is not a "modern person." Although Hume accurately points out in his examples that *some* people in certain ages tended to believe in miracles more than *some* people in other ages (which is a rather trivial observation),[23] one cannot deduce from this that *all* the people in a particular age were therefore gullible and believed in miracles on an insufficient basis. Furthermore, one could alternatively attack the modern age as being so bent on naturalism that it has become closed-minded to the supernatural; chronological snobbery cuts both ways.[24] Therefore, each miracle claim must be examined individually apart from any *ad hominem* generalizations. As Brown points out:

> It is absurd to demand of a witness that he should share the same world view as oneself or have the same level of education and culture. . . But the validity of the testimony to a claim *that* something happened depends rather upon the honesty, capacity not to be deceived, and proximity of the witnesses to the alleged event.[25]

MIRACLE STORIES OF CONFLICTING RELIGIONS CANCEL EACH OTHER OUT

Hume asserts that the miracle-claims in the different world religions serve as a foundation to demonstrate the truth of each particular religious system. However, he asks us to consider

> that, in matters of religion, whatever is different is contrary; and that it is impossible the religions of ancient Rome, of Turkey, of Siam and of China should, all of them, be established on any solid foundation. Every miracle, therefore, pretended to have been wrought in any of these religions (and all of them abound in miracles), as its direct scope is to establish the particular system to which it is attributed; so has it the same force, though more indirectly, to overthrow every other system.[26]

Thus, "in destroying a rival system, it likewise destroy the credit of those miracles, on which that system was established."[27] In a letter to Reverend Hugh Blair, Hume presents his argument with greater clarity: "If a miracle proves a doctrine to be revealed from God, and consequently true, a miracle can never be wrought for a contrary doctrine. The facts are therefore as incompatible as the doctrines."[28] Hence the miracle-claims in the different world religions (which have contradictory theological systems) are self-canceling.[29]

There are at least three problems with this criterion: (1) The most it does is devalue the stature of a miracle; (2) It assumes that all miracles are of equal *quality*; and (3) Hume would have a point *only* if most miracle claims are actually true. Concerning the first point, maybe it is true that most of the miracle-claims in contradictory religions have indeed occurred, but this goes to prove only that miracles *cannot* be cited as evidence of religious truth. That is all. Hume does not impugn the *actuality* of miracles *per se*. However, if we intend to hold to a particular view of God in our definition of a miracle (e.g., "a miracle is brought about by the only true God, and this God alone."), then all the miracles in other religions which hold contrary and exclusive concepts of God, if they in fact have occurred, do cancel each other out in terms of their apologetic value (i.e., "This miracle is evidence that this belief-system is God's,"). On the other hand, this does not mean that any one of these anomalous *events* did not occur, or that a disembodied rational being may not have brought about any one of them; that is, it may be that the gods of two different religions may both exist, and are responsible for miracles within their own respective spheres (human beings may have mistakenly dogmatized their own particular god). Therefore, at most this criterion is saying that there may be something wrong with our *explanations* for these events, not that these events have not occurred.

The second point asks the question: Is it correct to assume that all miracles are created equal, that one is *qualitatively* as good as another? I do not think so. For example, the Christian religion claims that its founder conquered man's most detestable foe (death) in order to demonstrate the truth of his claims. We submit that it is a qualitatively greater accomplishment, because of its obvious existential significance and human impossibility, to conquer death than to perform another type of miracle. Hume admits to the significance of death in the following passage from his *Natural History of Religion*:

> We are placed in this world, as in a great theatre, where the true springs and causes of every event are entirely concealed from us; nor have we either sufficient wisdom to foresee, or power to prevent those ills, with which we are continually threatened. *We hang in perpetual suspense between life and death, health and sickness, plenty and want; which are distributed among the human species by secret and unknown causes, whose operation is oft unexpected, and always unaccountable.*[30] (emphasis mine)

Albert Camus' sobering and profound observation serves as a gentle reminder of the Grim Reaper's deftly approaching shadow:

> Likewise and during every day of an unillustrious life, time carries us. But a moment always comes when we have to carry it. We live in the future: "tomorrow," "later on," "when you have made your way," "you will understand when you are old enough." Such irrelevancies are wonderful, for, after all, its a matter

of dying. Yet a day comes when a man notices that he is thirty. Thus he asserts his youth. But simultaneously he situates himself in relation to time. He takes his place in it. He admits that he stands at a point on a curve that he acknowledges having to travel to its end. He belongs to time, and by the horror that seizes him, he recognizes his worst enemy. Tomorrow, he was longing for tomorrow, whereas everything in him ought to reject it. That revolt of the flesh is the absurd.[31]

Edward John Carnell also describes the situation most accurately:

The incongruity between man's desire for life and the reality of physical death is the most maddening problem of all. Although he sees the handwriting on the wall, man yet refuses to think that death is his final destiny, that he will perish as the fish and the fowl, and that his place will be remembered no more. Man wills to live forever; the urge is written deep in his nature.[32]

Someone may argue that there are religious views (e.g., Taoist) which seem relatively unconcerned about death. But this begs the question. For it seems to me that such religious views do *not* say that death is the cessation of existence, but a spiritual passage from one state of existence to another. Hence, these religious views, by explaining death in this way, actually show that death as personal annihilation is existentially repugnant and serve as further evidence that death is man's worst enemy.

By virtue of this universally accepted truth, we can conclude that a religion which is grounded on the miracle of a physical resurrection from the dead, has in its apologetic arsenal a qualitatively better miracle than any other religious system has yet to put forth. This type of miracle touches man at his deepest existential and personal level, and can be a source of hope, assurance, and peace of mind if the person who conquered death promises eternal life to those who follow his teachings. Therefore, Hume is wrong on this point, miracle-claims do not cancel each other out, but must be examined as to their quality and, of course, whether they have actually occurred or not.

This brings us to our third point: Hume's observation is well-taken only if most miracle claims have actually occurred. Habermas writes:

Hume's fourth criterion states that the miracle claims of many different religions cancel out rival ideologies. But such a criterion would only be valid only if all miracle claims were *true* That one religion may back its revelation claims with invalid "miracles" is no reason to reject a religion possessing valid claims. Inept systems cannot cancel a religion that may be supported by evidence that is shown to be probable. Since obviously not all miracle claims are valid, historical investigation into evidential claims in a theistic universe is needed to ascertain if any religion has a probable basis.[33]

In other words, it may be the case that religion A and religion B, contradictory religious systems, each claim that God has ordained its teachings as true via miraculous events. And given the fact that there is good evidence that the miracles of each religion have occurred, and they are qualitatively equivalent, they would surely cancel each other out. However, let us suppose that religion A has little or no evidence for its miracles, while the miracles of religion B have very convincing evidence in their favor. If this is the case, then the miracles of religion A and religion B do not cancel each other out, simply because there is little or no evidence that the miracles of religion A have occurred. And, of course, if the miracles of religion A and religion B are evidentially equal, and religion A claims to be ordained by the true God because its leader has the ability to instantaneously heal patterned baldness, while religion B appeals to the resurrection of its founder, then religion B has a qualitatively better miracle.

Given the fact that miracles are qualitatively different and that they are not of equal evidential value, there still is a question, implied in Hume's fourth criterion, which we should address in this book: If an event occurs that we believe to be a miracle, is it ever reasonable to say that it has a divine source? In addition to what we have gone over in this section, the following two points should help us to answer this question: (A) The problem of causality; and (B) The religious context and teleological element of a miraculous event.

The Problem of Causality

As we noted in the second chapter, according to Hume, attributing a cause to a particular event is dependent upon the regularity of the conjunction of the two events. For example, the reason why I may say that billiard ball A caused billiard B to move is because the regularity of my experience leads to the belief that the latter object is moved by the former. Although I cannot *rationally*, in a Cartesian sense, prove that billiard ball A caused billiard B to move, my experience (based on constant conjunction and custom, etc.) prompts me to infer that such is the case (that it is "reasonable" to believe in). Hence, Hume uses the term "reasonable" (or "rational") in two different senses. T.E. Jessop points out that what Hume means by *reasonable* in the latter context is a conclusion derived from the process of associatively determined causal inference, a process which, because it is not logical but natural, he assigns in his more careful moments of writing to the imagination. It is, of course, reason in this shockingly loose sense that he asserts to be a "slave of the passions." Reason in the strict sense "mortifies" them--or, rather, would do in a perfectly pure philosopher, which, he implies, no one can become.[34]

Robert J. Roth points out that Hume may use "reasonable" in a *third* way:

> But I would suggest that Hume slips into still another meaning, perhaps inadvertently, when he says that his position is "the only reasonable account we can give of necessity." Reasonable here does not mean that which is in accord with logical relations or imaginative associations but that which in the long run makes sense.[35]

I am more inclined to think that this "third" sense of "reason" in Hume is a species of his non-logical, or second, use of reason. However, regardless of whether there are two or three senses of reason in Hume, the domain in which it is reasonable to believe something on the basis of evidence is referred to by Hume as the realm of *natural beliefs*: those beliefs that we cannot *rationally* justify (in a Cartesian sense) but are *practically* necessary for us to function properly in the everyday world.[36] And it is within this sense of the word "reasonable" that we shall work in responding to the problem of causality (among other topics) as it relates to miracles.

Hume himself saw the practical consequences of a rejection of causality and other natural beliefs (although he does not refer to it as such, Hume's Cartesian assumption is most evident):[37]

> But allow me to tell you, that I never asserted so absurd a Proposition as *that any thing might arise without a Cause*: I only maintain'd, that our Certainty of the Falsehood of that Proposition proceeded neither from Intuition nor Demonstration; but from another Source. *That Caesar existed, that there is such an Island as Sicily*; for these Propositions, I affirm, we have no demonstrative nor intuitive Proof. Woud you infer that I deny their Truth, or even their Certainty? There are many different kinds of Certainty; and some of them as satisfactory to the Mind, tho perhaps not so regular, as the demonstrative kind.[38]

Nature is always too strong for principle. And though a

58

Pyrrhonian may throw himself or others into a momentary amazement and confusion by his profound reasonings; the first and most trivial event in life will put to flight all his doubts and scruples, and leave him the same, in every point of action and speculation, with the philosophers of every other sect, or with those who never concerned themselves with philosophical researches. When he awakes from his dream, he will be the first to join in the laugh against himself, and to confess, that all his objections are mere amusement, and can have no other tendency than to show the whimsical condition of mankind, who must *act and reason and believe*; though they are not able, by their most diligent enquiry, to satisfy themselves concerning the foundation of these operations, or to remove the objections, which may be raised against them.[39] (emphasis mine)

The advantage of discussing Hume's position on miracles within the confines of practical reasonableness is that this is the very context in which Hume presents his argument. Hume does *not* argue that miracles are impossible because they allegedly take place in the external world, and since one cannot rationally demonstrate the reality of the external world, the miraculous is irrational (along with everything else that is not a relation of ideas). Rather, it seems obvious that Hume assumes the practical undeniability of natural beliefs and argues from that vantage point.

Applying Hume's epistemology to the miraculous, it can be asked: since the cause of a miracle is said to be a god, and a miracle is a unique non-recurring event, how is it possible for the believer to reasonably infer that a god is responsible for this event? In other words, there appears to be no constant conjunction in experience between a god and a particular miraculous event (such as in the case of the billiard balls).

In response, the believer in miracles agrees with Hume that constant conjunction between two events must be the *basis* for making empirical judgments regarding a causal relationship. However, he disagrees with Hume that such a conjunction between a god and an event must be the reason for belief in miracles. For example, if while combing the Nevada desert I come across an abandoned stone object resembling Socrates and similar to objects that I call works of art or sculpture, I would reasonably infer that it was designed by a rational being. This judgment is reasonable, according to Humean epistemology, simply because of the constant conjunction of my experience, which asserts that objects and events with design and purpose are brought about by rational beings. However, let us say that while in the desert that same day I am visited by rational non-human beings from another world. Although I have no previous experience with such beings (and hence, constant conjunction cannot be the *object* of my knowledge), I know they are rational beings simply because of how they are acting in front of me; they are doing things that rational beings do. Of course, I *could* be wrong (only to demonstrate Hume's assertion that we cannot know the necessary connection between matters of fact), but I am entirely within my epistemic rights, *based* on the constant conjunction of my previous experience, to infer that these are rational beings. Carl Sagan, in discussing the possibility of receiving intelligent communication from extraterrestrials, provides us with another example along the same lines (although I am sure he did not intend this as a defense of miracles):

> There are others who believe that our problems are soluble, that humanity is still in its childhood, that one day soon we will grow up. The receipt of *a single message from space* would show that it is possible to live through such technological adolescence: the transmitting civilization has survived. Such knowledge, it seems to me, might be worth a great price.[40] (emphasis mine)

Although I have had no experience of extraterrestrial communication, I have had experience of *rational* communication. Hence, a single message from outer-space, possessing the earmarks of rationality, is sufficient for me to reasonably infer that I am receiving communication from a rational being. Undergirding this whole notion is the assumption that present *regularities* can serve as the basis from which we can infer past or present *singularities*. An excellent example of this thinking is the formulation of the "big bang" cosmology. Norman L. Geisler and J. Kerby Anderson write:

> Although some scientists believe the big bang is only the most recent explosion in an endless series of explosions and contractions, a current body of evidence supports the scientific model of a beginning of the universe. The second law of thermodynamics affirms that in a closed isolated system (such as the whole universe) the amount of usable energy is decreasing. So it is argued that even if the universe did have enough mass to rebound, nevertheless, like a bouncing ball in reverse, it would rebound less and less until it could rebound no more. Thus, according to big bang cosmogony, the regular laws of the universe (thermodynamics, measurable expansion) point to a unique singular beginning.
>
> Whether or not the big bang theory is correct is not the point here. What is significant is that a scientific hypothesis has been developed in which the regularities of the present are used as a key to formulating a scientific view suggesting a past singularity of origin. Without these

observable laws there would be no way to construct a scientific model bout a past observed singularity. So regularities (constant conjunctions) in the present are the key to a scientific approach to the singularity in the past. By using observed regularities from the present it is possible to construct a scientific model about a past singularity which has no parallel in the present.[41]

The believer in miracles is stating that a miracle is a singular non-recurring event which can be reasonably attributed to a rational disembodied being because of its designed purpose, religious context, and human impossibility. As we have seen in the above examples, the fact that we have not experienced a constant conjunction of rational non-human beings does not mean that such cannot be reasonably inferred from experience (just as we have not experienced singular "big bangs," although it is perfectly reasonable to infer such a singular event). Since we know from experience that messages, or other sorts of intelligent communication, come from rational beings, it is highly likely that a miracle is brought about by a rational being if there is a message or purpose conveyed by the very occurrence of the event. Furthermore, since our experience dictates that human beings are incapable of producing most miraculous events (such as resurrections), a miraculous event is one which is brought about by a rational being with powers beyond that of a human being.

Of course, Hume could say that all our experiences with rational beings have been with those who have bodies, and since a god is defined as a disembodied rational being, a god cannot be responsible for a so-called miraculous event. But clearly this is question-begging. If our experience has given us a foundation from which we can make particular inferences, we must follow the evidence where it leads us (just as scientists do in the case of big bang cosmology, and may possibly do in the case of an extraterrestrial message). As Swinburne writes:

> So if because of very strong similarity between the ways and circumstances which effects are produced by human agents, we postulate a similar cause--a rational agent--the fact that there are certain disanalogies (viz. we cannot point to the agent, say where his body is) does not mean that our explanation is wrong. It only means that the agent is unlike humans in not having a body. But this move is only justified if the similarities are otherwise strong.[42]

Geisler and Anderson write that "if a single event conveys specifically complex information, then it may be assumed to have a primary (intelligent) cause." Furthermore, "a naturalist has no scientific grounds for assuming a present singularity is naturally caused unless it can be shown to be part of a recurring pattern of events. If it can, then by definition, it has a secondary cause [i.e., natural cause]. But if it is not known to be part of a regular recurring pattern then it may have a primary cause [i.e., supernatural cause]." Hence, "what is necessary for a theist to establish a singularity as a miracle is to show that it fits into a complex information-conveying context." Therefore, "if it can be shown to convey specified and complex information, then by analogy (the principle of uniformity) the theist has justification to posit a primary cause for it."[43]

Teleological Significance and Religious Context

Design, purpose, and context are helpful in determining the meaning of events in all aspects of life. For example, the sound of a slamming door after a heated quarrel with one's spouse conveys a message (and meaning) which would not be present if no quarrel had taken place. A cold piercing stare from an angry Larry Bird after a called foul in the middle of a hotly contested ballgame against the Lakers communicates a message which would be incapable of being clearly understood apart from the context. However, in neither one of these cases is there a logical connection between event and meaning (or message). It could very well be that the slamming door after a marital quarrel was caused by an unexpected gust of wind. In the case of Mr. Bird, it may be that he was thinking about a quarrel he had with his wife in the afternoon prior to the Lakers game. Nevertheless, the fact that well-founded beliefs are corrigible does not take away from the reasonableness of such beliefs. For such corrigibility has not detained such disciplines as science, law, and history from making reasonable judgments. Therefore, one would be entirely within one's epistemic rights to infer from both the context of the event and the event itself that a particular message is being communicated.

In light of what we have gone over in both the problem of causality and the above paragraph, consider the following example. Suppose that a purported miracle-worker, C, says that he is God's chosen and that he will perform a miracle, R, a resurrection, at time *t* in order to confirm God's approval on his mission. Furthermore, C is vehemently opposed by the religious elite who insist that he is *not* God's chosen. Moreover, every person who has ever made claims similar to C's has remained dead (and this also goes for those who will make these claims afterwards). Therefore, if C performs R at *t*, it seems entirely reasonable to believe that C is God's chosen one. Given its human impossibility, its uniqueness (i.e., nobody who has made similar claims, except C, has ever performed R), C's claim that God is responsible for R, its existential and teleological significance (i.e., C performed R at a particular time *t*, not at any other time), and the religious context of the event (i.e.,

C performed R when his claims about himself hinged on the actuality of R occurring at time *t*), it becomes apparent that a particular message is being communicated through this event, namely, *C is God's chosen one.* Hence, a god's presence as the rational agent responsible for this occurrence, although not incorrigible, most adequately accounts for both the event and the message conveyed by this event. Furthermore, in light of the *converging* nature of the facts in this case, and the inference to a rational cause made eminently plausible by them, any appeals to *coincidence* or *freak accident* become entirely *ad hoc*, a sort of naturalism-of-the-gaps.

Leon Pearl cites the miracles described in the Bible as examples of events that demand a non-natural rational cause:

> The marvels in the Bible have three features: they are often predicted; they collectively form goal directed patterns; they are witnessed by many. The following is an instance illustrating these features. A voice claiming to be God predicted to Moses that terrible plagues would shortly afflict Egypt; the prediction came true. The plagues appeared to be goal directed, toward the liberation of the Israelites from the bondage of Egypt and their arrival in the promised land. These occurrences were not only witnessed by Moses, but also by his brother Aaron, his follower Joshua and by others (both Israelites and Egyptians) as well. These three features (prediction, being goal oriented and public observation) are to be found not only in *Exodus* but throughout biblical narrative. This consideration makes it highly unlikely that the reports of the marvelous occurrences were the result of illusion, fraud or mere coincidences and thus renders it highly probable that a superhuman entity brought about the incredible events recorded in the Bible.[44]

Although it is of tremendous importance whether any or some biblical-type miracles have actually occurred, it is simply my intention in this chapter to argue that *if* such events have taken place, *then* the believer in miracles would be within his epistemic rights in postulating a rational cause for such events.

Summarizing the Critique of Hume's Fourth Criterion

Hume's assertion that miracles in contrary religious systems cancel each other out is incorrect for at least three reasons. First, it does not prove that miracles did not happen, but just impugns their faith-proving value. Second, it incorrectly assumes that all miracles are qualitatively the same. And third, this criterion is really only applicable if in fact there is evidence that many miracle-claims in contrary religious systems have actually occurred (i.e., if there is good evidence for miracles in only one particular religious tradition, Hume's problem does not arise).

Taking this criterion one step further, the question was asked: If an event occurs which we believe is a miracle, is it ever reasonable to say that it has a divine source? In response to this question we examined two areas of concern. First, we analyzed the problem of whether it is possible to infer a singular cause without the benefit of observing a constant conjunction of cause and effect. Far from being impossible, we saw that to infer a singular cause from particular regularities is perfectly reasonable (e.g., the big bang theory). Second, we saw that it is also reasonable to infer that a miracle came about by the power of a rational non-human cause (i.e., a god), on the basis of the miracle's purpose, timing, existential significance, religious context, and human impossibility. Just as in the case of inferring a singular empirical cause from particular empirical regularities (e.g., the big bang theory), a god is inferred from certain earmarks of rationality which we have derived from the regularities of our experience. If, of course, one can show that it is rational to believe in God's existence apart from inferring God from the miraculous, one has a stronger case for believing that God has acted. For one would then be within one's epistemic rights in believing that there exists a God who *could* perform miracles. In the next chapter I present a case for the rationality of belief in God apart from the miraculous.

NOTES FOR CHAPTER FOUR

[1]J.C.A. Gaskin, *Hume's Philosophy of Religion* (London: Macmillan, 1978), pp. 115-116.

[2]David Hume, *An Enquiry Concerning Human Understanding*, 3rd edition, text revised and notes P.H. Nidditch, intro. and analytic index L.A. Selby-Bigge (Oxford: Clarendon, 1975; reprinted 1777 edition), p. 116.

[3]*Ibid.*, pp. 116-117.

[4]Colin Brown, *Miracles and the Critical Mind* (Grand Rapids, Mich.: Eerdmans, 1984), p. 97.

[5]Among the facts of Christ's Resurrection which are accepted as historical by a virtually unanimous number in the scholarly community, the following seem to fulfill Hume's criterion: (1) The Resurrection occurred in a major metropolis, Jerusalem; (2) The event is attested to by a sufficient number of good witnesses; and (3) These witnesses were adequately educated. Concerning points (1) and (2), nearly all scholars agree that Jesus died by crucifixion in Jerusalem, and soon afterwards a good number of people claimed to have had experiences with the risen Christ. See James D.G. Dunn, *The Evidence For Jesus* (Philadelphia: Westminster, 1985), p. 75; Gary R. Habermas in *Did Jesus Rise From the Dead?: The Resurrection Debate*, ed. Terry L. Miethe (New York: Harper & Row, 1987), pp. 15-32; Gary R. Habermas, *Ancient Evidence For the Life of Jesus* (New York: Thomas Nelson, 1984); Gary R. Habermas, *The Resurrection of Jesus* (Lanham, MD: University Press of America, 1980), pp. 21-42; and Wolfhart Pannenberg, *Jesus--God and Man*, trans. L.L. Wilkens and D. Priebe (Philadelphia: Westminster, 1968). Concerning point (3), William L. Coleman writes: "Many Jews, especially around the first century A.D., received a good 'liberal arts' education, thanks to the influence of Babylon, Greece, and Rome. Nonetheless, they spent much of their energies in maintaining their religious heritage. To this extent, education was vital and the people received an excellent education. They were literate early in their history because of a simple alphabet and that literacy was among the masses at least by the time of Joshua. We may be tempted to assume that populations 2,000 years ago were fairly ignorant. Regarding some subjects this was true, but in many areas they had amazing knowledge and ability to apply that knowledge. When we mention the Jews of the first century, we are talking about an intelligent people with a keen appreciation for education." (William L. Coleman, *Today's Handbook of Bible Times and Customs* [Minneapolis: Bethany House, 1984], pp. 101-102).

In addition to these points, it should be noted that certain facts, although not demonstrating the historicity of the Resurrection, converge upon the event so as to make it more probable: (4) The tomb of Jesus was empty; (5) The disciples of Jesus were willing to suffer martyrdom and torture because of what they allegedly had witnessed; and (6) The naturalistic explanations of the event (e.g., the swoon theory, the stolen-body theory, etc.) are wholly inadequate. See Karl Barth, *Church Dogmatics*, ed. G.W. Bromiley and T.F. Torrance, 13 vols. (Edinburgh: T. and T. Clark, 1961), 4 (part one): 340; William Lane Craig, "The Empty Tomb," in *Gospel Perspectives II*, ed. R.T. France and David Wenham (Sheffield, England: JSOT Press, 1981); Habermas in *Did Jesus Rise From the Dead?*, pp. 25-27; Habermas, *Ancient Evidence*, pp. 54-58; Habermas, *Resurrection*, pp. 21-42; Gary R. Habermas, *The Resurrection of Jesus: A Rational Inquiry* (Ann Arbor, Mich.: University Microfilms, 1976), pp. 114-171; and Robert H. Stein, "Was the Tomb Really Empty?" *Journal of the Evangelical Theological Society*, 20 (March 1977): 23- 29.

[6]See Gaskin, *Hume's Philosophy of Religion*, pp. 105-125.

[7]Sherlock's work is photocopied in *Jurisprudence: A Book of Readings*, ed. John Warwick Montgomery (Strasbourg: International Scholarly Publishers; Orange, CA: Simon Greenleaf School of Law, 1974), pp. 339-459.

[8]Hume, *Enquiry*, pp. 124-125.

[9]Richard Swinburne, *The Concept of Miracle* (New York: Macmillan, 1970), p. 16.

[10]Hume, *Enquiry*, pp. 117-119. Hume makes similar points, concerning the evolution of religion, in his *Natural History of Religion* (in *Hume Selections*, ed. Charles W. Hendel, Jr. [New York: Charles Scribner's Sons, 1927], pp. 257-258): "An historical fact, while it passes by oral tradition from eye-witnesses and contemporaries, is disguised in every successive narration, and may at last retain by very small, if any, resemblance of the original truth, on which it was founded. The frail memories of men, their love of exaggeration, their supine carelessness; these principles, if not corrected by books and writings, soon pervert the account of historical events. . ."

[11]A good example is the so-called miracles of Mormonism: Joseph Smith's miraculous "translation" of the golden plates of the *Book of Mormon*; allegedly fulfilled prophecy; assorted visitations by angelic beings; etc. See Walter R. Martin, *The Maze of Mormonism* (Santa Ana, CA: Vision House, 1978). Among his many observations, Martin points out that the *Book of Mormon* has no basis in archaeology, history or anthropology (*Ibid.*, pp. 46-69), that Mormonism is riddled with false prophecies (*Ibid.*, pp. 352-359), and that the miraculous appearances of angels to Joseph Smith were unconfirmed by other witnesses (*Ibid.*, pp. 26-30, 38-40). See also, Jerald and Sandra Tanner, *The Changing World of Mormonism*

(Chicago: Moody, 1980)

[12]Vincent E. Barry and Douglas J. Soccio, *Practical Logic*, 3rd ed. (New York: Holt, Rinehart and Winston, 1988), p. 200.

[13]Brown, *Miracles*, p. 97.

[14]Swinburne, *Concept*, p. 17.

[15]*Ibid.*

[16]Hume, *Enquiry*, pp. 119-121.

[17]Swinburne, *Concept*, p. 17.

[18]*Ibid.*

[19]*Ibid.*

[20]*Ibid.*

[21]Hume, *Enquiry*, p. 124.

[22]Barry and Soccio, *Practical Logic*, p. 93.

[23]Hume, *Enquiry*, pp. 120-121. For example, some people assume that the people in Jesus' day were necessarily gullible and that alleged miracle workers were found everywhere and in great numbers. For this reason, it is claimed that the miracles of Jesus were invented to conform with those allegedly performed by Jewish and pagan miracle workers. For an excellent critique of this criticism of the Christian miracles, see A.E. Harvey, *Jesus and the Constraints of History* (Philadelphia: Westminster, 1982), pp. 98-119. See also, Stephen T. Davis, "Is it Possible to Know that Jesus was Raised from the Dead?" *Faith and Philosophy*, 1 (April 1984): 156-157.

[24]In the detailed syllabus for his Fuller Seminary course, "Signs and Wonders," Rev. John Wimber has made the observation that the "Western worldview has a blindspot which keeps most Westerners from dealing with or understanding problems related to spirits, ancestors, or anything supernatural." (John Wimber, "Today's Tension with the Miraculous: Worldview," section 3 of *Signs and Wonders and Church Growth* [Placentia, CA: Vineyard Ministries International, 1984], p. 1).

[25]Brown, *Miracles*, p. 98.

[26]Hume, *Enquiry*, p. 121.

[27]*Ibid.*

[28]J.Y.T. Greig, ed., *The Letters of David Hume*, 2 vols. (Oxford: Clarendon, 1932), I: 350-351.

[29]There are, of course, some religious systems which claim that the major world religions have an underlying unity. For example, the Baha'is teach that all the great founders of the major religions in world history (e.g., Jesus, Muhammed, Krishna, etc.) are manifestations of the same God. For a presentation and critique of this religious position, see Francis J. Beckwith, *Baha'i* (Minneapolis: Bethany House, 1985).

[30]Hume, *Natural History of Religion*, p. 262.

[31]Albert Camus, "Absurd Walls," in *Phenomenology and Existentialism*, ed. Robert C. Solomon (Lanham, MD: University Press of America, 1980), pp. 490-491.

[32]Edward John Carnell, *An Introduction to Christian Apologetics: A Philosophical Defense of the Trinitarian-Theistic Faith* (Grand Rapids, MI: Eerdmans, 1948), pp. 24-25.

[33]Gary R. Habermas, "Skepticism: Hume," in *Biblical Errancy: An Analysis of Its Philosophical Roots*, ed. Norman L. Geisler (Grand Rapids, MI: Zondervan, 1981), pp. 41-42.

[34]T.E. Jessop, "Some Misunderstandings of Hume," in *Hume*, ed. V.C. Chappell, Modern Studies in Philosophy Series (Notre Dame, IN: University of Notre Dame Press, 1966), p. 52. See also, Norman Kemp Smith, "The Misunderstandings due to Hume's Employment of the Term 'Reason' in two very different Senses," in chapter IV of his *The Philosophy of David Hume* (London: Macmillan, 1941), pp. 99-102.

[35]Robert J. Roth, "Did Peirce Answer Hume on Necessary Connection?" *Review of Metaphysics*, 38 (June 1985): 879. See Hume, *Enquiry*, p. 35.

[36]Gaskin writes that "Hume distinguishes at least three 'species of natural instincts' or 'natural beliefs':
    (1) Belief in the continuous existence of an external world independent of our perceptions of that world (*Enquiry*, 151: 160, etc.)
    (2) Belief that the regularities which have occurred in our experience form a reliable guide to those which will occur.
    (3) Belief in the reliability of our senses qualified to take account of acknowledged and isolatable areas of deception and confusions

(many locations)." (Gaskin, *Hume's Philosophy of Religion*, p. 132).

[37]Flew writes that Hume buys into the Cartesian "assumption that all arguments must be either deductive or defective, since the only sufficient reasons for believing any propositions are (other) propositions which entail it." (Antony Flew, *David Hume: Philosopher of Moral Science* [New York: Basil Blackwell, 1986], p. 17).

[38]*Letters of David Hume*, I: 187. This was written to John Stewart in 1754.

[39]Hume, *Enquiry*, p. 160. In the *Dialogues Concerning Natural Religion* (ed. and intro. Norman Kemp Smith [New York: Bobbs-Merrill, 1947; originally published, 1779], p. 134), Philo asserts the following, which is never questioned by any of the other participants in the dialogue: "To whatever length any one may push his speculative principles of skepticism, he must act, I own, and live, and converse like other men; and for this conduct is not obliged to give any other reason than the absolute necessity he lies under of so doing."

[40]Carl Sagan, *Broca's Brain* (New York: Random House, 1979), p. 275.

[41]Norman L. Geisler and J. Kerby Anderson, *Origin Science* (Grand Rapids, Mich.: Baker Book House, 1987), p. 117.

[42]Swinburne, *Concept*, p. 58.

[43]Geisler and Anderson, "Miracles and Primary Causality," appendix 3 of *Origin Science*, pp. 171-172.

[44]Leon Pearl, "Miracles: The Case for Theism," *American Philosophical Quarterly*, 25 (October, 1988): 336

CHAPTER FIVE

THE RATIONALITY OF BELIEF AND THE EXISTENCE OF GOD

Although Hume in his miracles chapter does not argue for the impossibility of divine intervention on the basis that there is no independent evidence that a divine being exists,[1] a number of contemporary philosophers argue that one cannot identify an act of God unless one already knows that such a being exists.[2] Since my intention in this work is to deal with both Hume's argument and its contemporary rehabilitations, I think this question of the existence of a god should be dealt with. Furthermore, since Hume's fourth criterion states that miracle-claims of contradictory theological systems cancel each other out, the number of miracle-claims which we must examine would be lessened if it could be shown that the god of a particular theological system is more likely to exist than any other. Although I believe that what we have covered thus far in terms of identifying the miraculous is sufficient, it seems reasonable to believe that if there is good reason to assert that there exists a particular god who can perform miracles, it makes it more plausible to believe that a god may have miraculously intervened in a particular situation which seems to communicate a certain message.

However, prior to presenting an argument for God's existence I want to first examine Alvin Plantinga's argument that belief in God is rational apart from any evidence. If Plantinga is correct, then the theist, in order to be within his intellectual rights, has no epistemic obligation to fulfill the non-theist's demand for evidence of God's existence prior to ascribing a divine source to a supposedly miraculous event.

THE RATIONALITY OF BELIEF IN GOD

Plantinga argues against what he calls the evidentialist objection to belief in God.[3] Evidentialists argue that unless a proposition is either fundamental to knowledge or based on evidence, one is not rationally justified in believing the truth of the proposition in question. Hence, according to evidentialism, since the proposition "God exists" is not foundational to knowledge, it is not rational to believe that God exists unless one has sufficient evidence. However, Plantinga asks why the proposition "God exists" is not foundational to knowledge and thus not in need of evidence. The typical evidentialist response is that only *properly basic* propositions are foundational to knowledge. But

71

how do we know which propositions are properly basic? The evidentialist usually replies that the only properly basic propositions are those which are self-evident and incorrigible. An example of a self-evident proposition is "All squares have four sides." An example of an incorrigible truth would be "I feel pain." For even if my pain is imaginary it is nevertheless incorrigibly true that I do feel pain. Hence it follows that since the proposition "God exists" is not self-evident or incorrigible, it is not properly basic. And if it is not properly basic, one needs evidence if one wants to rationally believe in God. Therefore, belief in God, apart from evidence, is irrational.

Plantinga responds by asking how we know that self-evident and incorrigible propositions are the only ones that are properly basic. After all, cannot the believer in God point out to the evidentialist that the proposition "only propositions that are self-evident and incorrigible are properly basic" is itself not properly basic because it is neither self-evident nor incorrigible. And neither is it supported by evidence. Furthermore, if evidentialism is true,

> then enormous quantities of what we all in fact believe are irrational. . . [R]elative to propositions that are self-evident and incorrigible, most of the beliefs that form the stock in trade of ordinary everyday life are not probable. . . Consider all those propositions that entail, say, that there are enduring physical objects, or that there are persons distinct from myself, or that the world has existed for more than five minutes; none of these propositions, I think, is more probable than not with respect to what is self-evident or incorrigible to me.[4]

Therefore, evidentialism results in affirming that a number of beliefs which we consider to be rationally acceptable are in fact not rational at all. That is why Plantinga points out that many propositions that the evidentialist ought to reject based on his test for proper basicality

> are properly basic for me. I believe, for example, that I had lunch this noon. I do not believe this proposition on the basis of other propositions; I take it as basic; it is in the foundations of my noetic structure. Furthermore, I am entirely rational in so taking it, even though this proposition is neither self-evident nor evident to the senses nor incorrigible for me.[5]

Therefore, since it is apparent that the evidentialist's criterion is inadequate, he cannot rule out *a priori* the possibility that belief in God is properly basic. Thus Plantinga writes that the evidentialist criterion is no more than a bit of intellectual imperialism . . . He commits himself to reason and to nothing more; he therefore declares irrational any noetic structure that contains more--belief in God, for example, in its foundation. But here there is no reason for the theist to follow his example; the believer is not obliged to take his word for it. So far we have found no reason at all for excluding belief in God from the foundations; so far we have found no reason at all for believing that belief in God cannot be basic in a rational noetic structure. To accept belief in God as basic is clearly not irrational in the sense of being proscribed by reason or in conflict with the deliverances of reason. The dictum that belief in God is not basic in a rational noetic structure is neither apparently self-evident nor apparently incorrigible.[6]

Furthermore, Plantinga clarifies his position by pointing that just because belief in God is properly basic it does not logically entail that *any* belief is properly basic, nor does it entail that belief in God is *groundless.*[7] Although both these clarifications are important to his case, I will not present them here. My chief reason for citing Plantinga's argument is to merely show that the theist is *not* irrational if she does not *prove* God's existence prior to ascribing a divine agent to a supposed miraculous event. Hence, Plantinga's position is strictly negative. Therefore, if the theist wants to convince or persuade a non-theist of God's existence, a positive case should be developed.

THE KALAM COSMOLOGICAL ARGUMENT

Although there are various arguments for God's existence within the confines of the four traditional argument-types (i.e., the cosmological, teleological, ontological, and moral arguments), there is one particular form of the cosmological argument which I find to be very convincing, namely, *the kalam cosmological argument.*[8]

The kalam cosmological argument gets its name from the word *kalam*, which refers to Arabic philosophy or theology. The kalam argument was popular among Arabic philosophers in the late Middle Ages. Christian philosophers during that period did not generally accept the argument, perhaps due to the influence of Aquinas, who, following Aristotle, rejected it. A notable exception was Saint Bonaventure, a contemporary of Aquinas, who argued extensively for the soundness of the kalam argument.[9]

Despite the fact that it is not demonstrable in any Cartesian sense, I believe that it is an argument which is entirely reasonable within the realm of Hume's *natural beliefs*, and avoids all of the pitfalls of the Thomistic and Leibnizian cosmological arguments as pointed out by Hume and others.[10] That is to say, although belief in God is *not* a natural belief for Hume (i.e., one can function most adequately without belief in God), I will argue that *given* these natural beliefs one can reasonably infer the fact that there exists a god. Furthermore, given the fact that it is perfectly legitimate to infer a singularity from certain regularities (as evidenced by the possibility of extraterrestrial communication and the big bang cosmology, see chapter 4), it is not *a priori* irrational to infer a first cause from certain given regularities. Therefore, if one rejects the kalam argument, one must reject natural beliefs, but since it is entirely unreasonable and woefully impractical to do so, one must reject the kalam argument for reasons other than merely rejecting it because natural beliefs are not rationally demonstrable (that is, their rejection does not involve a *logical* contradiction). The argument can be put in the following form:

1. Everything that begins to exist does so only through a cause.

2. The universe had a beginning.

3. Therefore, the universe has a cause, of which we can infer particular attributes.

Craig offers the following diagram:[11]

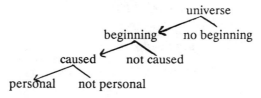

This argument is presented as a series of alternatives. First, it is asserted that the universe either had a beginning or it did not. Secondly, if the universe in fact had a beginning, then it was either caused or uncaused. And thirdly, if the beginning of the universe was caused, then this cause was either personal or impersonal. In showing one part of each alternative to be more reasonable than the other, this argument intends to show the reasonableness of believing in the existence of a personal Creator. Let us briefly examine each one of the premises of this argument.[12]

Everything that Begins to Exist does so Only Through a Cause

As we noted earlier, Hume insisted that he "never asserted so absurd a proposition as that anything might arise without a cause." He "only maintain'd, that our certainty of the falsehood of that proposition proceeded neither from intuition nor demonstration; but from another source."[13] This is such an obvious aspect of our human experience that no jury will accept an alibi from a burglar who claims that the stolen goods the police found in his appartment just popped into existence from nowhere. Nor will an angry wife, having found her husband in bed with another woman, accept the rather dubious excuse, "She just appeared out of nothing." Simply put, nothing does not produce something.

Although it is one thing to say that one is able to *imagine* without contradiction that something was produced by nothing, it is quite another thing to demonstrate how it is a *real* possibility that something can come into existence uncaused. Concerning this point, G.E.M. Anscombe writes:

> The trouble about it is that it is very unconvincing. For if I say I can imagine a rabbit coming into being without a parent rabbit, well and good: I can imagine a rabbit coming into being, and our observing that there is no parent rabbit about. But what am I to imagine if I imagine a rabbit coming into being without a cause? Well, I just imagine a rabbit coming into being. That this *is* the imagination of a rabbit coming into being without a cause is nothing but, as it were, the *title* of the picture. Indeed I can form an image and give my picture that title. But from my being about to do *that*, nothing whatever follows about what is possible to suppose 'without contradiction or absurdity' as holding in reality.[14]

In essence Anscombe is arguing that it does not follow from my imagining a rabbit coming into existence without a cause that in fact it is really possible to suppose that something can arise uncaused. That is to say, since it is always possible that something that appears to have arrived uncaused may in fact have a cause we are unaware of, one must eliminate every possible cause in order to demonstrate that something has come into existence without a cause. But since such a task is impossible, one cannot say that something came into existence without a cause. In response, David Gordon writes that just because "we cannot tell whether something has come into existence without a cause is no reason against thinking that such a circumstance is possible."[15] Gordon states that just as one can never know enough in order *to prove* that something has come into existence uncaused, it is likewise never possible to possess enough data *to rule out* the possibility that something has come into existence uncaused (i.e., it is always possible that something has come into existence uncaused).[16] Hence, Anscombe's argument cuts both ways and does not rule out the possibility that something can come into existence uncaused.

What are we to think of this objection? First, it does not refute, but merely calls into question, the *a priori* truth of the assertion that something does not arise from nothing. One can always retort by asserting that the principle that "something cannot arise from nothing" is an *a posteriori* truth repeatedly confirmed and never refuted by millenia of human experience, although we cannot rule out *a priori* that something can arise from nothing. Second, and this follows from the first point, Gordon merely states that it is *logically* possible that something could come from nothing, *not* that it is *metaphysically* possible that non-being can produce being if being began to exist at some point (which is the essence of the causality principle defended herein). And third, Craig writes that because the "empirical evidence of the proposition [the causal principle] is absolutely overwhelming, so much so that Humean empiricists could demand no stronger evidence in support of any synthetic proposition. . .," a rejection of "the causal principle is therefore completely arbitrary."[17] Therefore, since it has not been demonstrated that it is plausible, reasonable, or intuitively obvious to reject causality (in fact, just the opposite is the case), and since within the confines of Humean "natural beliefs" causality is a necessity, there is every reason to suppose that this first premise is correct: everything that begins to exist does so only through a cause.

The Universe Had a Beginning

There are three options concerning the beginning of the universe: (a) the universe began to exist, but it was produced by nothing; (b) the universe had no beginning, and has therefore always existed; and (c) the universe began to exist, but it was produced by something outside itself. Since we saw in our first premise that everything begins to exist does so only through a cause, to claim that (a) is true is to utter an absurdity.[18] Given the absurdity of (a), maybe (b) is true--the universe never began to exist. However, this option also has its problems. Craig has developed several arguments which explain why the universe must have had a beginning.[19] We will take a close look at one of them, and briefly summarize another. Craig presents the former in the following way:[20]

1. The series of events in time is a collection formed by adding one member after another.

2. A collection formed by adding one member after another cannot be actually infinite.

3. Therefore, the series of events in time cannot be actually

infinite.

The first premise seems rather indisputable. For when we think of the series of events in time we do not think of them as happening all at the same time, but happening one after another. For example, despite the tasteless jokes at bachelor parties, one's wedding and one's funeral do not happen at the same time: the first precedes the second (one hopes with a large number of years in between).

In the second premise we are arguing that "a collection formed by adding one member after another cannot be actually infinite." An *infinite set* of numbers is one that is complete and cannot be added to, e.g., the infinite set of natural numbers {1,2. . . 10. . .1,000,000. . .}. This set contains an *unlimited* number of digits from 1 to infinity. However, since an actual infinite is a *complete* set with an infinite amount of members, the series of events in time cannot be actually infinite. This is because the series of events in time is always increasing (being added to) and one can never arrive at infinity by adding one member after another. The following example should help to demonstrate this.

If you were on Interstate 15 driving from Los Angeles to Las Vegas with 280 miles to cross, there is no doubt that you will eventually arrive in Las Vegas. However, if you were to drive on an Interstate 15 from L.A. to Las Vegas with an infinite number of miles to cross, you will never arrive in Las Vegas. But if you did arrive in Las Vegas, it would only prove that the distance was not infinite. Since an infinite number is unlimited, one can never complete an infinite number of miles.

Applying all this to a universe with no beginning, a certain absurdity develops: if the universe had no beginning, then every event has been preceded by an infinite number of events. But if one can never arrive at infinity by adding one member after another, one could never arrive at the present day, because to do so one would have to "cross" (or complete) an infinite number of days to arrive at the present day. J.P. Moreland writes:

> . . . suppose a person were to think backward through the events in the past. In reality, time and the events within it move in the other direction. But mentally he can reverse that movement and count backward farther and farther into the past. Now he will either come to a beginning or he will not. If he comes to a beginning, then the universe obviously had a beginning. But if he never could, even in principle, reach a first moment, then this means that it would be impossible to start with the present and run backward through all of the events in the history of the cosmos. Remember, if he did run through all of them, he would reach a first member of the series, and the finiteness of the past would be established. In order to avoid this conclusion, one must hold that, starting

from the present, it is *impossible* to go backward through all of the events in history.

But since events really move in the other direction, this is equivalent to admitting that if there was no beginning, the past could have never been exhaustively traversed to reach the present.[21]

It is interesting to note that Hume admits to the impossibility of an infinite series of events in the past, although he does not consider it in relation to this argument:

An infinite number of real parts of time, passing in succession, and exhausted one after another, appears so evident a contradiction, that no man, one should think, whose judgement is not corrupted, instead of being improved, by the sciences, would ever be able to admit it.[22]

Because contemporary philosophy has been unable to refute this argumentation, non-theistic philosophers have found the above reasoning somewhat disquieting.[23] For example, John Hospers writes:

If an infinite series of events has preceded the present moment, how did we get to the present moment? How could we get to the present moment--where we obviously are now--if the present moment was preceded by an infinite series of events?[24]

Craig points out that science has also been helpful in confirming that the universe had a beginning. He asserts that the second law of thermodynamics reveals the impossibility of an infinite past. The second law can be defined in the following way: ". . . the whole universe must eventually reach a state of thermodynamic equilibrium; everywhere the situation will be exactly the same, with the same temperature, the same pressure, etc., etc."[25] An example of how this functions can be seen when you put some ice cubes in a glass with a warm soda. Both the soda and the ice cubes tend toward the same temperature: the ice cubes begin to melt and the soda gets a bit cooler. Just think of this on a cosmic scale and you will get an idea of what the second law is asserting: the universe is running down and will inevitably reach heat death.

Applying this to the question of the beginning of the universe, the following can be asked: If the universe is moving toward a point when everything will be the same temperature, why has it not occurred if the universe has had no beginning? If the universe has always existed, there certainly has been enough time (infinite time) for this to have occurred. But since this has not occurred, it is obvious that the universe has had a beginning.[26] Given the soundness of both our philosophical and scientific arguments, the conclusion is vindicated: the series of events in time cannot be actually infinite.

Prior to moving on to our conclusion, we should make mention of several objections to the kalam argument. We will first look at two classical arguments, and then we will look at some contemporary ones. Probably the most famous classical arguments come from Thomas Aquinas' defense of his admission that there is no clear philosophical proof for creation in time, since God could have created from all eternity.[27] Although Aquinas presents several arguments for this admission, I will focus on the two which have direct bearing upon the kalam argument. First, he asserts that creation from all eternity does not involve a logical contradiction. Secondly, Aquinas argues that an infinite series of events in the past is possible. Concerning the first assertion, Thomas argues:

> First of all, no cause that produces its effect instantaneously has to precede its effect in time. Now, God is a cause that produces his effect, not through movement, but instantaneously. Hence he does not have to precede his effect in time. . . What is more, if there is ever a cause whose proceeding effect cannot co-exist at the same instant, the only reason would be the absence of some element needed for a complete causing; for a complete cause and its effect exist simultaneously. But God has never been incomplete. Therefore an effect caused by him can exist eternally, as long as he exists, and hence he need not precede it in time. . . Hence, although God is recognized as an agent acting voluntarily, yet it follows that he can see to it that what he causes should never be non-existent.
>
> And thus it is evident that no logical contradiction is implied in the statement that an agent does not precede its effect in time. God cannot, however, bring into being anything that implies logical contradiction.[28]

Several comments are in order. First, Aquinas' argument is certainly no option for the non-theist. That is, the addition of an omnipotent being, God, who alone is able to bring about an eternal creation, as a way out of a finite past, serves to demonstrate theism, not atheism. Second, the defender of the kalam argument is not arguing against the possibility of eternal creation, but against the possibility of an infinite series of events in the past; the two are not synonymous. As James Sadowsky has stated:

> It should be pointed out that this argument [the kalam argument] would not prove the non-eternity of the world to one

who did believe in God. Such an individual could while granting the world has not been eternally in action still claim that until God moved it from inaction to action, it had existed from all eternity in a purely static condition.[29]

Therefore, the real obstacle is Aquinas' second argument, which, if valid, could be of help to the non-theist who disputes the kalam argument. In defending the possibility of an infinite past, Aquinas argues in one place that one is attacking a straw man when one argues that because an infinite series cannot be traversed there cannot be an infinite series of events in the past. This is so because it "is founded on the idea that, given two extremes, there is an infinite number of mean terms." But the passage of time "is always understood as being from term to term." That is to say, "whatever by-gone day we choose, from it to the present day there is a finite number of days which can be traversed."[30] Bernardino Bonansea explains Aquinas' objection as saying that since there was no first moment in an eternal world, "no infinite distance is being traversed."[31]

Actually, the fact that there was no first moment really is of no help, and is entirely irrelevant. For instance, no doubt that when I discuss in 1988 the events of 1978, I make the judgment that the events of 1978 occurred 10 years ago and that a finite number of days have been traversed. The same goes for events that occurred 50, 100, or three million years ago. What Aquinas is arguing for is that no matter how far back one goes one will only be traversing a finite distance, and hence, one is not claiming to traverse an infinite. But this seems to vindicate our argument. For if one cannot in principle reach a day which occurred an infinite number of days ago--which is what Aquinas means when he asserts that "whatever by-gone day we choose, from it to the present day there is a finite number of days which can be traversed"--this only goes to prove the impossibility of traversing an actual infinite, which is the same thing as saying that all the events in the beginningless past could not have been crossed to reach today. Therefore, I do not see how Aquinas can effectively dispute our conclusion that a beginningless series of events in time is impossible.[32]

Among the contemporary philosophers who have disputed the kalam argument are J.L. Mackie, William Wainwright, and Richard Sorabji. I will briefly cover what I believe are their strongest arguments. Both Mackie and Wainwright present an argument nearly identical to Aquinas' second argument above.[33] Mackie writes that the kalam argument "assumes that, even if past time were infinite, there would still have been a starting-point in time, but one infinitely remote, so that an actual infinity would have had to be traversed to reach the present from there." However, Mackie points out that "to take the hypothesis of infinity seriously would be to suppose that there was no starting-point, not even an infinitely remote one, and that from any specific point in past time there is only a finite stretch that needs to be traversed to reach the present."[34]

Like Aquinas' second argument, this one is also weak. First, as Moreland states, the defender of the kalam argument "does *not* assume an infinitely distant beginning to the universe to generate his puzzles against traversing an actual infinite."[35] That is to say, the problems involved in traversing an actual infinite occur precisely because there is no beginning. As I pointed out in the critique of Aquinas' argument, if one cannot in principle reach a day which occurred an infinite number of days ago, this only goes to prove the impossibility of traversing an actual infinite. Second, it seems that Mackie and Wainwright are arguing that because each finite segment of an infinite series can be in principle traversed, a whole infinite series made up of finite segments can also be traversed. But this commits the informal fallacy of division, which occurs when someone mistakenly argues that what is true of the part is also true of the whole. For example, just because each part of my car is light, does not mean that the entire care as a whole is light. Thus it is Mackie and Wainwright who do not take the infinite seriously.

Sorabji argues that our objection to an infinite past makes the mistake of confusing counting with traversing. He writes that it is impossible to count to infinity if one begins at a particular starting point. But an infinite past has *no* starting point. Therefore, it is possible that an infinite past has been traversed.[36]

Several comments are in order. First, as Moreland points out, the criticisms against traversing an actual infinite are based on the *nature* of the actual infinite, *not* on the nature of counting. That is to say, whether one is talking about either starting a count from one or a beginningless series of events, it is an actual infinite number that is alleged will be or has been traversed.[37] Second, how does not having a starting point make an actual infinite suddenly traversable? Is it not true that an infinite series with a starting point and an infinite series with no beginning have the same amount of members? Why then is traversing the latter less difficult than traversing the former? Moreland presents the following example:

> . . . assume that someone had been counting toward zero from negative infinity from eternity past. If a person goes back in time from the present moment, he will *never* reach a point when he is finishing his count or even engaging in the count itself. This is because at every point, he will have already had an infinity to conduct the count. As Zeno's paradox of the race course points out, the problem with such a situation is not merely that one cannot complete an infinite task; one cannot even start an infinite task from a beginningless situation. For one could never reach a determinate position in the infinite series which alone would allow the series to be

traversed and ended at zero (the present moment).[38]

Hence, the absence of a beginning makes traversing an actual infinite even worse. As Craig has observed, such a task is like trying to jump out of a bottomless pit. Although there are other criticisms of this portion of the kalam argument, they seem to be derived from the ones we have already covered. I refer the reader to the works which deal with these criticisms.[39]

Therefore, the Universe has a Cause, of which We Can Infer Particular Attributes

In the first premise of this argument we found that everything that begins to exist does so only through a cause. The second premise showed us that the universe had a beginning. Therefore, since the universe had a beginning and everything that begins to exist does so only through a cause, it follows that the universe has a cause. Given this inference, I believe that we can reasonably infer that this cause possesses certain attributes.

First, this cause must be an *uncaused being*. This cause can only be one of there types of being: (a) self-caused; (b) caused by another; or (c) uncaused. It cannot be self-caused, because then it would have to exist before it existed. Just as a son cannot be his own father, a being cannot be the cause of its own existence. Furthermore, this cause cannot be caused by another. If it were caused by another, we could in turn ask: "What caused this cause?" and so on and so on. But since we have already demonstrated that there cannot be an infinite series of events in the past, there *must* be a cause which is uncaused. In other words, you have got to stop somewhere once you realize that you cannot stop with the universe itself (i.e., it has a beginning and therefore demands a cause outside itself). Hence we are left with only one option: there must exist an uncaused cause.

Secondly, this cause must have been *changeless*. Since change does not occur except through the agency of another (i.e., every effect demands a cause), and the cause of the universe is uncaused, it logically follows that this cause was changeless. As Geisler has observed:

> . . . since nothing does not give rise to something on its own, it follows that the only possible way a substantial change could occur is if there were some ground of being beneath the change, making it possible for something to appear where there was nothing.[40]

Thirdly, this cause is an *eternal being*. Since this cause is uncaused, it must also be eternal. That is, if there was a time when this cause did not exist, nothing would exist at the present moment. However, the finite universe does exist, and it therefore follows that this cause must be an eternal being. Think about it: How can an uncaused cause come into existence if it is not eternal? (What would cause it to be?) Therefore, this cause must be an eternal being.

Moreover, although this cause is eternal, its existence could *not* consist of a beginningless series of past events, a series which we have seen is impossible. That is to say, since this cause was changeless prior to creation and there cannot be any time without change (i.e., one event succeeding another in time), this cause was simply timeless prior to creation. As Craig puts it:

> Prior to creation, there was no time at all, for time cannot exist unless there is change. God Himself is changeless; otherwise you would find an infinite series of past events in His life, and we know that such an infinite series is impossible. So God is changeless, and hence, timeless prior to creation.[41]

Therefore, since there was no time or change prior to the beginning of the universe, and hence no series of events, there was no infinite series of past events in the existence of this cause.[42] Furthermore, it would appear that if this cause was eternal and changeless at the moment ontologically prior to the first event, there is no reason to suppose that this being ceased to exist afterwards. Actually, the burden of proof is on the one who asserts that it is possible that an immutable and eternal being can cease to exist. Such a possibility is extremely unlikely, if not logically impossible.[43]

Fourthly, this cause must be a *personal* or *rational* being (see also note 42). Arguing for this attribute, Craig asks: "How can a first event come to exist if the cause of that event has always existed? Why isn't the effect as eternal as the cause?"[44] For example, if a high pollen count is the cause of my sneezing, and if there has been a high pollen count for all eternity, I would be sneezing from all eternity. But as Craig has pointed out, "the only way to have an eternal cause but an effect that begins at a point in time is if the cause is a *personal agent* who freely decides to create an effect in time."[45] For example, a man who has been resting for all eternity may will to create a work of art; "hence, a temporal effect may be caused by an eternally existing agent."[46] Concurring with Craig, Moreland writes:

> If the necessary and sufficient conditions for a match to light are present, the match lights spontaneously. There is no deliberation, no waiting. In such situations, when *A* is the efficient cause of *B*, spontaneous change or mutability is built into the situation itself.

The only way for the first event to arise spontaneously from a timeless, changeless, spaceless state of affairs, and at the same time be caused, is this--the event resulted from the free act of a person or agent. In the world, persons or agents spontaneously act to bring about events. I myself raise my arm when it is done deliberately. There may be necessary conditions for me to do this (e.g., I have a normal arm, I am not tied down), but these are not sufficient. The event is realized only when I freely act. Similarly, the first event came about when an agent freely chose to bring it about, and this choice was not the result of other conditions which were sufficient for that event to come about.[47]

Therefore, the only way out of this problem is to conclude that this cause *willed* the universe to come into existence at a temporal moment. And since "will" is an attribute of a rational or personal being, this cause must be personal.

In conclusion, we can state that the kalam argument has shown that it is entirely reasonable to assert that there exists a personal, eternal, and changeless creator of the universe. Only one title is befitting of a being possessing such attributes: God. Furthermore, because it affirms both the impossibility of an infinite series of events in the past and the ontological necessity of a first cause outside this series of events, the kalam argument excludes from consideration world-views which assume a universe with an infinite past, such as process philosophy,[48] some forms of finite godism, polytheism, and pantheism. Hence, any miracle claims which are ascribed to any of these "gods" should be held suspect from the outset, simply because all the evidence points to the fact that it is highly unlikely that such "gods" actually exist.[49]

NOTES FOR CHAPTER FIVE

[1]However, it seems that Hume was moving toward this position when he wrote: "Though the Being to whom the miracle is ascribed, be, in this case, Almighty, it does not, upon that account, become a whit more probable; since it is impossible for us to know the attributes or actions of such a Being, otherwise from the experience which we have of his productions, in the usual course of nature." (David Hume, *An Enquiry Concerning Human Understanding*, 3rd edition, text revised and notes P.H. Nidditch, intro. and analytic index L.A. Selby-Bigge [Oxford: Clarendon, 1975; reprinted from the 1777 edition], p. 127).

[2]For example, see Antony Flew, *God: A Critical Enquiry*, 2nd ed. (LaSalle, IL: Open Court, 1984), pp. 143-148; and Norman L. Geisler, *Miracles and Modern Thought* (Grand Rapids, MI: Zondervan, 1972), pp. 62-75.

[3]Among the number of works in which Plantinga has put forth his case are the following: Alvin Plantinga, *God and Other Minds* (Ithaca, NY: Cornell University Press, 1968); Alvin Plantinga, "Is Belief in God Rational?" in *Rationality and Religious Belief*, ed. C.F. Delaney (Notre Dame, IN: University of Notre Dame Press, 1979); Alvin Plantinga, "Rationality and Religious Belief," in *Contemporary Philosophy of Religion*, eds. Stephen M. Cahn and David Shatz (New York: Oxford University Press, 1982); and Alvin Plantinga, "Reason and Belief in God," in *Faith and Rationality: Reason and Belief in God*, eds. Alvin Plantinga and Nicholas Wolterstorff (Notre Dame, IN: University of Notre Dame Press, 1983).

Two works that have helped me to better understand and appreciate Plantinga's position are William Lane Craig's *Apologetics: An Introduction* (Chicago: Moody Press, 1984), pp. 16-17, and Ronald Nash's *Faith and Reason: Searching for a Rational Faith* (Grand Rapids, MI: Zondervan, 1988), pp. 69-92. Because of Plantinga's influence, I have changed my view to a moderate evidentialism and no longer hold to the narrow foundationalism I defended in my earlier writings (see my *Baha'i* [Minneapolis: Bethany House, 1985], pp. 42-43, and "Does Evidence Matter?," *Simon Greenleaf Law Review: A Scholarly Forum of Opinion Interrelating Law, Theology and Human Rights*, 4 [1984-85]: 231-235).

[4]Plantinga, "Reason and Belief in God," pp. 59, 60.

[5]*Ibid.*, p. 60.

[6]Plantinga, "Is Belief in God Rational?," p. 26.

[7]See Plantinga, "Rationality and Religious Belief," pp. 270-277, and Plantinga, "Reason and Belief in God," pp. 74ff.

[8]The chief advocate and most articulate defender of the kalam argument is William Lane Craig. His initial work on the topic is *The Kalam Cosmological Argument*, Library of Philosophy and Religion Series (New York: Barnes & Noble, 1979). A popular and much briefer version of this work is entitled, *The Existence of God and the Beginning of the Universe* (San Bernardino, CA: Here's Life Publishers, 1979). Subsequent works which deal with objections to his original work include *Apologetics*, pp. 73-93; "*Creation ex nihilo*," in *Process Theology*, ed. Ronald H. Nash (Grand Rapids, MI: Baker Book House, 1987), pp. 41-73; "Philosophical and Scientific Pointers to Creation ex Nihilo," *Journal of the American Scientific Affiliation* 32 (March 1980): 5-13; and "Professor Mackie and the Kalam Cosmological Argument," *Religious Studies* 20 (1985): 367-375. See also, James Sadowsky, review of *The Kalam Cosmological Argument*, by William Lane Craig, *International Philosophical Quarterly* 21 (June 1981): 222-223.

[9]J.P. Moreland, *Scaling the Secular City* (Grand Rapids, MI: Baker Book House, 1987), p. 18. Moreland defends Craig's argument. See also, William Lane Craig, *The Cosmological Argument from Plato to Leibnitz*, Library of Philosophy and Religion series (New York: Barnes & Noble, 1980).

[10]See David Hume, *Dialogues Concerning Natural Religion*, ed. and intro. Norman Kemp Smith (New York: Bobbs-Merrill, 1947), section IX, pp. 188-192; Paul Edwards, "The Cosmological Argument," in *The Cosmological Arguments: A Spectrum of Opinion*, ed. Donald R. Burrill (Garden City, NY: Doubleday & Co., 1967); Antony Flew, *God: A Critical Inquiry*, 2nd ed. (LaSalle, IL: Open Court, 1984), pp. 76-92; and William L. Rowe, "Two Criticisms of the Cosmological Argument," in *Logical Analysis and Contemporary Theism*, ed. John Donnelly (New York: Fordham University Press, 1972).

[11]Craig, "Philosophical and Scientific Pointers," p. 5.

[12]Needless to say, because of the topic of this book, I will not be able to present this argument in its most detailed and elaborate form. For such a presentation I suggest Craig's books (see note 8) and Moreland, *Scaling*, pp. 18-42.

[13]*Letters of David Hume*, I:187.

[14]G.E.M. Anscombe, "'Whatever Has a Beginning Of Existence Must Have a Cause': Hume's Argument Exposed," *Analysis*, 34 (April 1974): 145. See also, G.E.M. Anscombe, "Times, Beginnings, and Causes," in *Rationalism, Empiricism, and Idealism: British Academy Lectures on the History of Philosophy*, ed. Antony Kenny, (Oxford: Clarendon, 1986), pp. 86-103.

[15]David Gordon, "Anscombe on Coming into Existence and Causation," *Analysis*, 44 (March 1984): 54.

[16]*Ibid*, pp. 53-54.

[17]Craig, *Kalam*, p. 145.

[18]There are some thinkers, believe it or not, such as Isaac Asimov and Paul Davies, who argue that the universe could have come into being from nothing, if nothing is defined as the balance of positive and negative energy. Because their arguments rest on a confusion of what actually constitutes nonbeing, Moreland's remarks should suffice:
"If a state of zero energy *is* conceived of as nothing, then *it* does not exist. Nothingness has no nature and thus it has no exigency or internal striving toward the production of *any* state of affairs, much less one where positive and negative energy is balanced. . . Nothingness has no properties whatever, and it is not identical to an existent state of affairs where the positive and negative charge, or the positive and negative energy, is equal. The latter contains some sort of stuff (protons and electrons or energy); the former contains nothing."
"It is, then, a mistake to use language like that of Asimov and Davies. Such talk seems to say that nonbeing is identical to an existent state of affairs with positive and negative properties. But nothingness is just that, and nothingness has no nature, no causal powers, or tendencies toward anything whatsoever."
"One suspects that at bottom, the assertion that the universe came from nothing without a cause is a mere assertion without support; a sort of ungrounded logical possibility which provides the atheist with a last-ditch effort to avoid the existence of a first Cause. Atheist B.C. Johnson asserts that 'if time might have been nonexistent [prior to the first event], then so might causality. The universe and time might have just popped into existence without a cause.' Such a view is a logical possibility, but one which is most likely metaphysically impossible, and in any case, one without sufficient reasons. There is no reason to deny what we experience as true every day. Events have causes. So did the first one." (Moreland, *Scaling*, p. 41)

[19]Craig uses four arguments to show that the universe began to exist. The first two arguments are philosophical, the last two are empirical. (1) The first "is based upon the impossibility of the existence of an actual infinite." (2) The second is an "argument from the impossibility of the formation of an actual infinite by successive addition." (3) The third is an "argument from the expansion of the universe." (4) The fourth is an "argument from thermodynamics." (Craig, *Kalam*, pp. 69, 102-103, 111, 130). In this book the second argument will be presented, nd the fourth argument will be briefly summarized.

[20]Craig, *The Existence of God*, p. 49.

[21]Moreland, *Scaling*, p. 29.

[22]Hume, *Enquiry*, p. 157.

[23]For example, after presenting St. Bonaventure's cosmological argument, William L. Rowe remarks, "It is difficult to show exactly what is wrong with this argument," and then he goes on to present Leibniz's argument. (William L. Rowe, *The Cosmological Argument* [Princeton, NJ: Princeton University Press, 1975], p. 122)

[24]John Hospers, *An Introduction to Philosophical Analysis*, 2nd ed. (London: Routledge & Kegan Paul, 1967), p. 434.

[25]P.J. Zwart, *About Time* (Oxford: North Holland Publishing, 1976), p. 136.

[26]Although there are several objections to this argument, the following two are the most forceful: (1) The universe oscillates back and forth from eternity, and (2) The universe is infinite. Craig responds to (1):
"Some scientists have tried to escape this conclusion by arguing that the universe oscillates back and forth from eternity, and so never reaches a final state of equilibrium. . . The fact is that the thermodynamic properties of this model imply the very beginning of the universe that its proponents seek to avoid. For as several scientists have pointed out, each time the model universe expands it would expand a little farther than before. Therefore, if you traced the expansions back in time they would get smaller and smaller and smaller. . . As another writer points out, this implies that the oscillating model of the universe still requires an origin of the universe prior to the smallest cycle." (Craig, *Apologetics*, p. 90).
Concerning objection (2), Moreland writes:
". . .it has been argued that the universe is infinite and, therefore, the argument does not work. The universe could be infinite in two ways relevant to this objection: either it is infinite in extension and in the matter/energy present in it, or it is finite but there is a constant creation of new energy from an infinite source of energy or from nothingness. This objection runs aground on the problems already raised with an actual infinite [see Moreland, *Scaling*, pp. 22-28]. Furthermore, the most widely accepted current understanding of the universe is one which views it as finite and not infinite. And there is no scientific evidence for continuous creation of matter or energy, even if such a notion could be squared with the highly rational principle that something cannot come from nothing without a cause." (Moreland, *Scaling*, pp. 35-36).

Also responding to (2), Craig writes:
"Even if the universe were infinite, it would still come to equilibrium. As one scientist of the University of London [P.C.W. Davies] explained in a letter to me, if every finite region of the universe came to equilibrium, then the whole universe would come to equilibrium. This would be true even if there were an infinite number of finite regions. This is like saying that if every part of a fence is green, the whole fence is green, even if there are an infinite number of pickets in the fence. Since every finite region in the universe would suffer heat death, so would the entire universe." (Craig, *The Existence of God*, p. 67).

[27]Thomas Aquinas, "On the Eternity of the World against the Grumblers," as found in *An Aquinas Reader*, ed. and intro. Mary T. Clark (Garden City, NY: Image Books, 1972), pp. 178-185; and Thomas Aquinas, *Summa Theologica*, I, 46, as found in *Introduction to St. Thomas Aquinas*, ed. and intro. Anton C. Pegis (New York: The Modern Library, 1948), pp. 246-258.

It should be noted that Aquinas himself does not believe in eternal creation. He is merely asserting that since there is no clear philosophical proof against it, the Christian can only believe in a beginning of time on the basis of faith, as he does with the doctrine of the Trinity. See *Summa Theologica*, I, 46. 2.

[28]Aquinas, "Eternity of the World," pp. 180-181.

[29]Sadowsky, review of *Kalam*, p. 222. Of course, this "purely static condition" would be a condition completely unknown to contemporary science.

[30]Aquinas, *Summa Theologica*, I, 46. 2

[31]Bernardino Bonansea, O.F.M., "The Impossibility of Creation From Eternity According to St. Bonaventure," *Proceedings of the American Catholic Philosophical Association* 48 (1974): 124.

[32]Sadowsky cites another Thomistic objection: "Aquinas has a curious objection: he denies that an eternity of past events constitutes a completed infinity on the grounds that since the past no longer exists, it is not an actual infinity. But it is logically possible for each event to have left a permanent trace and that would surely involve the consummated infinite." (Sadowsky, review of *Kalam*, p. 222). Because of the inability this objection to seriously challenge our argument, I chose to deal only with the two which I believe really pose a threat.

[33]William Wainwright, review of *The Kalam Cosmological Argument* by William Lane Craig, *Nous*, 16 (May 1982): 328-334, and J.L. Mackie, *The*

Miracle of Theism (Oxford: Clarendon, 1982), p. 93.

[34]Mackie, *Miracle*, p. 93.

[35]Moreland, *Scaling*, p. 32.

[36]Richard Sorabji, *Time, Creation, and the Continuum* (Ithaca, NY: Cornell University Press, 1983), pp. 221-222.

[37]Moreland, *Scaling*, p. 32.

[38]*Ibid.*, pp. 31-32.

[39]For detailed responses to these other objections, see Craig, "*Creation ex nihilo*," pp. 163-166, and Moreland, *Scaling*, pp. 30-33.

[40]Norman L. Geisler, *Philosophy of Religion* (Grand Rapids, MI: Zondervan, 1974), p. 205.
The question that usually arises concerning immutability and the problem of miracles is: "How can an immutable God relate (sometimes through divine intervention, such as with miracles) to a changing world without Himself changing in some way?" In response, I propose the following: if one defines current changelessness as essential to God's nature, and not pertaining to any inability in His nature to act (and hence avoiding all the problems that go along with putting God in pure Aristotelian categories), then there seems to be no problem with saying that God is both changeless and able to relate to his creation. For example, W. Norris Clarke writes that "the immutability attributed to God must be that proper to a perfect personal being--i.e., an *immutable intention* to love and save us, which intention then includes all the adaptations and responses necessary to carry this intention through in personal dialogue with us. Thus *personal* immutability includes relational mutability." (W. Norris Clarke, *The Philosophical Approach to God* [Winston-Salem, NC: Wake Forest University Press, 1979], p. 108).

[41]Craig, *The Existence of God*, p. 87.

[42]Because of obvious space limitation we are incapable of dealing with the question of how the kalam argument relates to Kant's first antinomy. However, it is interesting to note that Craig sees the solution to this antinomy in the postulating of rationality (i.e., personhood) to the first cause of the universe (see text for the argument for the first cause's personhood):
"The antithesis of the first antinomy, which like the thesis echoes so clearly the arguments of the *mutakallimun*, really asks, why did the universe begin to exist when it did instead of existing from eternity?

The answer to Kant's conundrum was carefully explained by al-Ghazali and enshrined in the Islamic principle of determination. According to that principle, when two different states of affairs are equally possible and one results, this realisation of one rather than the other must be the result of the action of a personal agent who freely chooses one rather than the other. Thus, Ghazali argues that while it is true that no mechanical cause existing from eternity could create the universe in time, such a production of a temporal effect from an eternal cause is possible if and only if the cause is a personal agent who wills from eternity to create a temporally finite effect. For while a mechanically operating set of necessary and sufficient conditions would either produce the effect from eternity or not at all, a personal being may freely choose to create at any time wholly apart from any distinguishing conditions of one moment from another. For it is the very function of will to distinguish like from like. Thus, on a Newtonian view of time, a personal being could choose from eternity to create the universe at any moment he pleased. On a relational view of time, he could will timelessly to create and that creation would mark the inception of time." (Craig, *Kalam*, pp. 150-151). See also, "Appendix 2: The *Kalam* Cosmological Argument and the Thesis of Kant's First Antinomy," in *Ibid.*, pp. 189-205.

[43]Nash raises this objection when he asks us to imagine "a *very* long series of falling dominoes that might take fifty years to complete. Imagine someone who comes to the scene near the end, watches the last domino fall, and then wonders about the First Cause of this series. While such a person might be justified in believing that the causal series in question had a First Cause, it might well be the case--given the long period of time involved--that the being whose action caused the first domino to fall no longer existed." (Nash, *Faith and Reason*, p. 123).

[44]Craig, *The Existence of God*, p. 86.

[45]Craig, *Apologetics*, p. 93.

[46]*Ibid.*

[47]Moreland, *Scaling*, p. 42.

[48]For example, see William Lane Craig's critique of process theology, "*Creation ex nihilo*."

[49]For example, Mormonism holds that certain miracles validate Joseph Smith's claim that he is God's prophet, who is supposed to restore "true" Christianity. However, Mormonism's view of God as a finite being (who was once a man and eventually attained godhood through eternal progression)

in a polytheistic and eternal universe, which has an infinite series of events in its past, makes Smith's claims (regardless of their theological and Biblical problems) tremendously implausible from the outset. See Bruce R. McConkie, "Beginning," in his *Mormon Doctrine*, 2nd ed. (Salt Lake City: Bookcraft, 1966, pp. 76-77, and Sterling M. McMurrin, *The Philosophical Foundations of Mormon Theology* (Salt Lake City: University of Utah Press, 1959). I have discussed this and another problem in my paper, "Two Philosophical Problems with the Mormon Concept of God," which was presented at the 40th annual meeting of the Evangelical Theological Society (November 19, 1988), Wheaton College, Wheaton, IL. A revised version of this paper ("The Mormon Concept of God: Two Philosophical Difficulties?") will be published in a forthcoming issue of the Mormon journal, *Sunstone*.

It should be noted, however, that "the traditional notion of miracle as a suspension of natural law is usually denied by Mormon writers in favor of the interpretation that an event is miraculous only in the sense that the causal laws describing it are unknown to us. . . From the divine perspective there are no miracles." (McMurrin, *Philosophical Foundations*, p. 19).

CHAPTER SIX

CONTEMPORARY REHABILITATIONS OF HUME'S ARGUMENT

As I noted earlier, the philosophical opposition to miracles did not end with Hume in the eighteenth century.[1] However, it is not until this century that we find an impressive quantity of philosophically sophisticated defenses of Humean-type arguments. In this chapter I intend to deal with the contemporary rehabilitations of Hume's argument which I believe are the strongest, as put forth by the following thinkers: Antony Flew, Alastair McKinnon, and Patrick Nowell-Smith. Because the arguments discussed in this chapter are within the Humean tradition, some of our observations will reiterate and supplement what was discussed previously in chapters 3 and 4.

ANTONY FLEW'S CASE AGAINST MIRACLES

Flew has written on the topic of miracles in a number of books and articles.[2] From these works I believe that one can find at least *three* particular arguments against belief in the miraculous,[3] all of which are in the spirit of Hume's classic argument. Let us examine each one individually.

Argument From Critical History

Flew has cogently summarized this argument in the following quotation:

> The basic propositions are: first, that the present relics of the past cannot be interpreted as historical evidence at all, unless we presume that the fundamental regularities obtained then as still obtain today; second, that in trying as best he may determine what actually happened the historian must employ his present knowledge of what is probable or improbable, possible or impossible; and third, since *miracle* has to be defined in terms of practical impossibility the application of these criteria precludes proof of a miracle.[4]

This can be better understood if put in the following outline:

1. The believer in miracles investigates history in order to demonstrate the actuality of miracles.

2. Only if we assume that the regularities of the present were also true of the past can we hope to know anything historically.

3. In order to gain knowledge of the past, the critical historian must employ his present knowledge of what is possible/impossible, probable/improbable.

4. A miracle is a highly improbable, practically impossible, event.

5. Therefore, miracles can not be known historically.

Since there is no doubt that historical investigation is necessary if one is to show that a past miracle has occurred, the believer in miracles does not dispute Flew's first premise. Consequently, since "without criteria there can be no discrimination. . . and hence no history worthy of the name,"[5]Flew's second and third premises should be left unchallenged. Concerning his fourth premise, the believer in miracles does not disagree with Flew that a miracle is a highly improbable or practically impossible event, although it seems that Flew does not adequately distinguish between logical impossibility and physical impossibility (see below). Nevertheless, if an event was not highly improbable in terms of physical law it would not merit the appellation of miracle.

It is evident, therefore, that the believer in miracles finds his opposition to Flew's argument in its conclusion. That is to say, although his premises are for the most part correct, it is our contention that Flew's conclusion does not *follow* from his premises.

Flew seems to have overlooked the fact that the criteria by which we judge the historicity of events are the *basis*, not the *object*, of our historical investigation. There is no doubt that Flew is correct when he asserts that "the critical historian, confronted with some story of a miracle, will usually dismiss it out of hand. . ."[6] If Flew means that the antecedent improbability of a miracle makes any claim of its occurrence highly doubtful prior to the examination of the evidence, the believer in miracles does not disagree. However, as we pointed out in our analysis of Hume's argument, since the criteria by which we evaluate testimony and evidence are also based on certain regularities,[7] there does not seem to be any way to rule out in prinicple the possibility that one may be justified in believing that a particular miracle has occurred based on the convergence of independent probabilities. In this sense, regularity, because it is the basis and not the object of historical investigation, can yield a singular result.

Flew, of course, believes that the antecedent improbability of a miraculous event can never be outweighed by the evidence without admitting that the event was not miraculous:

> Our sole ground for characterizing the reported occurrence as miraculous is at the same time a sufficient reason for calling it physically impossible. Contrawise, if ever we became able to say that some account of the ostensibly miraculous was indeed veridical, we can say it only because we know that the occurrences reported were not miraculous at all.[8]

The problem with this assertion is that it is simply question-begging. The believer in miracles, although defining a miracle as a violation of natural law and hence physically impossible,[9] argues that such a concept is *not* logically impossible. That is, I can imagine, without any logical contradiction, the actuality of such events as resurrections, levitations, instantaneous healings, etc. Unlike logically impossible objects, such as married-bachelors and square-circles, the actuality of physically impossible events cannot be ruled out *a priori*.

To summarize what we have covered in detail elsewhere, if an actual event cannot be subsumed under either a current or new scientific law, and it is unique and unrepeatable, it is perfectly coherent to say that in this instance the *physically impossible* is *historically actual*. Concurring, William Lane Craig writes that Flew's argument fails because he "has made an unwarranted identification between nomological (as he puts it, physical) possibility and real, historical possibility."[10] He continues:

> The assumption hidden behind this identification is that nomologically impossible events cannot occur or, in other words, that miracles cannot happen, which is question-begging, as that is precisely the point to be proved. . . If one wishes to talk about historical possibility or impossibility at all, these terms ought not to be defined in terms of scientific law, but in terms of historical evidence.[11]

Among the many examples Flew employs to defend his argument from critical history is one employed by Hume "in the footnote to the Section 'Of Miracles' where he quotes with approval the reasoning of the famous physician De Sylva in the case of Mademoiselle Thibaut:"[12]

> It was impossible that she could have been so ill as was 'proved' by witnesses, because it was impossible that she could, in so short a time, have recovered so perfectly as he found her.[13]

In employing this example, Flew is asserting that the miraculous nature of the event (i.e., its physical impossibility) makes it *always* unreasonable to believe that this event has occurred. However, since physical impossibility can not be equated with logical impossibility, to discount all evidence for an event on this basis alone is to reason *a priori*, and hence to beg the question.

For it is certainly conceivable that an antecedently improbable event may have enough evidence in its favor to make belief in its occurrence eminently reasonable (see chapter 3 for examples of such occurrences). This is because, as we pointed out earlier, the criteria and standards by which one weighs evidence are themselves based on regularities and probabilities. Therefore, if a number of independent probabilities converge upon an alleged miraculous event, and alternative naturalistic explanations are inadequate to explain the data (i.e., they are hopelessly *ad hoc* and question-begging), then it becomes entirely reasonable to believe that this miraculous event has occurred. In light of this, let us revise Flew's example by giving it a contemporary setting, a greater number of details, and placing a letter before each important fact.

Suppose that on a particular Sunday, (A) Mrs. D, a person stricken with rheumatoid arthritis for the past ten years, is (B) instantaneously healed of her ailment, which entails the complete reconstruction of her bone structure and complete elimination of her disease, not merely the temporary disappearance of the symptoms. (C) This occurred moments she was prayed for, in the name of a certain god, by her pastor in the presence of the entire congregation (about 500 people). (D) Given the nature of her illness and the inability for a scientific law to make the healing explicable, this occurrence is a violation of natural law. (E) There is no doubt that Mrs. D had been diagnosed properly. She had been receiving therapy for ten years for a condition which had been getting progressively worse: (F) she had lost the ability to walk properly, make a fist, or even grasp her husband's hand. In fact, at times, (G) she could only get along with a wheelchair. (H) And the sleepless nights of body-wrenching pain were almost unbearable. At time t, prior to the prayer, Mrs. D was experiencing all of the above symptoms. At time t_2, moments after the prayer, all of Mrs. D's symptoms had disappeared without a trace of the disease ever having been present. (I) The total elimination of the disease and the reconstruction of her entire bone structure was later confirmed the following week by a half-dozen awe-struck physicians who had treated Mrs. D scores of times for her arthritic condition.

To claim that the above did not happen because miracles are antecedently improbable and physically impossible is to miss the whole point of historical investigation, and to engage in special pleading for one sort of regularity (natural laws) while ignoring another (the basis of evidential criteria). Although the antecedent probability of the event occurring is very low, the pieces of evidence (A. . .I), which are themselves based on certain regularities (e.g., "It is highly improbable that a half-dozen doctors in this case could all be wrong in their diagnosis") are independent probabilities which converge upon the event and make it reasonable to believe that this event has occurred. Furthermore, the radical law-violating nature of the healing and the timing of the event make appeals to coincidence and psychosomatics appear question-begging and *ad hoc*.

Flew's argument can also be viewed as an accusation that the theist is inconsistent. Davis summarizes this interpretation in the following way:

> People who offer historical or probabilistic arguments in favor of the occurrence of a given purported miracle, Flew says, themselves presuppose the very regularity of nature and reliability of nature's laws that they argue against. Their position is accordingly inconsistent.[14]

To a certain extent Flew is correct. Believers in miracles do in fact assume regularities so that they can show that an irregular event has occurred. However, as Davis has pointed out, the employment of regularities to argue for the irregular "hardly shows that their position is inconsistent."[15] For example, the very fact that the theist employs regularities in order to identify the irregular is no more inconsistent than the concerned husband who on the basis of his wife's lifelong fidelity (i.e., the regular) is capable of identifying her singular act of infidelity (i.e., the irregular) when he finds her in bed with the mailman. Furthermore, if it were true that singular irregularities could not be discovered with a method which presupposes regularity, then scientists who believe in singular and non-analogous events, such as the "big bang," would be guilty of inconsistency and irrationality.[16]

As we asserted earlier, regularity must be the *basis*, *not* the object, of historical investigation, unless one is willing to reduce one's historical investigations to a question-begging enterprise, and hence eliminating true but irregular events from the outset. As Montgomery writes: "Unless we are willing to suspend 'regular' explanations at the particular points where these explanations are inappropriate to the particular data, we in principle eliminate even the possibility of discovering anything new."[17]

Argument From Explanation

In what one theologian called a "potent variation" of the above argument,[18] Flew writes that the believer in miracles must himself hold to some notion of regularity when he urges "that it is (psychologically) impossible that these particular witnesses [of the miraculous] were lying

97

or misinformed and hence that we must accept the fact that on this occasion the (biologically) impossible occurred."[19] Hence, the believer in miracles is arbitrary in his use of regularity.

Flew, of course, is making a cloaked reference to the traditional Christian apologetic for the Resurrection of Jesus.[20] The traditional apologist usually argues that it was psychologically impossible for Jesus' disciples (the eyewitnesses) to have knowingly lied about and suffered martyrdom for what they knew to be false, if in fact there was no Resurrection (e.g., the stolen body theory, the swoon theory, etc.). In addition, it would be equally absurd to believe that the other interest groups, the Jews and the Romans, had done something with the body of Jesus without later parading the corpse down the streets of Jerusalem in order to squash Christianity in its infancy. The Jews and the Romans, reasons the Christian apologist, would have acted outside of their own psychological make-up (not to mention, against their own interests) if they had done something with Jesus' body which would have given the disciples a reason to believe that their Master had risen from the dead (although an "empty tomb" in itself seems insufficient to warrant such belief, especially given the historicity of the post-resurrection appearances).[21]

In response, Flew asserts that the Christian apologist, in accepting the biological "miracle" and rejecting the psychological "miracle," holds to regularity when it suits his fancy (psychology)--i.e., "Nobody would die for what they knew to be false"--but rejects it when it conflicts with his own cherished beliefs (biology), i.e., "Dead men do not rise from the dead."

I believe that there are at least three problems with this argument. First, Montgomery has observed "that this argument seems somewhat inappropriate for the rationalist to propose."[22] He explains:

> Since he himself [the rationalist] is committed to employ only "ordinary" explanations of phenomena--explanations arising from "common experience"--he is in a particularly poor position to suggest any abnormal explanation for *any* aspect of a miracle account, including the psychological motivations or responses of the persons involved. Presumably the rationalist would be the last one to appeal to a "miraculous" suspension of ordinary psychology so as to permit the Jewish religious leaders (for example) to have stolen the body of Christ when they knew it to be against their own best interests.[23]

Second, this argument is subject to the same criticism that Flew levels against theists concerning their belief in God, namely, that it is *unfalsifiable* in principle. Flew has written that "it often seems to people who are not religious as if there was no conceivable event or series of events the occurrences of which would be admitted by sophisticated religious people to be sufficient reason for conceding 'there wasn't a God after all' or 'God does not really love us then'." He then poses the question to the theist: "What would have to occur or to have occurred to constitute for you a disproof of the love of, or the existence of, God?"[24] According to Flew, there does not seem to be any possible evidence that could disprove a believer's belief in God's existence. Hence, this belief is unfalsifiable and dies by a "death by a thousand qualifications. . ."[25]

However, in stating that the naturalist can reject what is an alleged biological miracle (such as a resurrection) by always appealing to a psychological "miracle" we can ask Flew the pointed question: What state of affairs would have to occur in order for you to accept a biological miracle or to falsify your naturalism? Unfortunately, this question is left unanswered.[26] This being the case, we can only conclude that in saying that it is epistemologically permissible for the naturalist to resort to the psychologically miraculous whenever there is good testimony for the biologically miraculous (presumably on the grounds that the theist is just as "arbitrary"), Flew holds to an unfalsifiable belief which in principle cannot be disproved. Therefore, judged by his own standards, Flew's position dies by a "thousand qualifications."

Third, Flew's position runs contrary to the proper goal of historical investigation, namely, to find the most *plausible* explanation of the alleged event based on the known *facts* of the case. Take for example the "facts" surrounding the alleged event to which Flew alludes, the Resurrection of Jesus. They assert that all the parties involved--the Jews, the Romans, and the disciples--acted just as one would expect them to act if such an event had in fact occurred. For instance, the Jews, after hearing of the Resurrection, are said to have bribed the Roman soldiers to say that the disciples had stolen the body. And the disciples, who were in the depths of despair following their Master's death, soon afterwards became bold martyrs for a faith they claimed was predicated upon Jesus' physical Resurrection. Such a reversal in attitude by more than a few individuals is psychologically inexplicable apart from a necessary and sufficient condition.[27]

However, Flew would have us believe that the Christian is arbitrary in accepting this scenario as lending credence to the actuality of the Resurrection, because one can alternatively say that all the parties involved were individually and collectively acting in a way that is psychologically "impossible". This is because for Flew it is perfectly acceptable to reject the historicity of the Resurrection solely on the basis that one would rather hold to one regularity ("dead people stay dead") than to the regularities on which evidential criteria are grounded (e.g., "people usually don't suffer martyrdom for what they know to be false.").

But this move only shows that Flew is the one guilty of arbitrariness, not the believer in miracles. For in the case of the

99

Resurrection, certain facts surrounding the event are bordering on historical certainty, for example: (1) Jesus died due to crucifixion; (2) the disciples had subsequent experiences of which they were convinced were literal appearances of the risen Jesus; (3) these men were transformed to bold martyrs; and (4) Paul's conversion experience was predicated upon what he believed was an appearance of the risen Jesus.[28] Adding to this the inadequacy of the naturalistic theories to disprove the historicity of the Resurrection[29] and the ever-increasing acceptance of the historicity of the empty tomb,[30] the critical historian is faced with the question of how he will properly view the alleged event in light of *these* known facts. And the question cannot be answered by simply saying, as Flew does, that the pieces of evidence (that is, the known facts) must be faulty because dead men do not rise. For to do so would be to beg the question. To put it simply, the historian must draw a conclusion *based* on these recognized facts, instead of imposing a naturalistic preference to avoid a supernatural conclusion.

The point I am making is *not* that historical facts may not warrant two or more equally plausible interpretations of an alleged event, but that the proper way to interpret an event is to find an explanation that is coherent and plausible in light of these facts and not to import explanations that are foreign to the data. Montgomery writes:

> Thus, in the argument for Christ's resurrection, nothing in the primary documents forces the historian to miraculous explanations of motives or actions of the Romans, the Jewish religious leaders, or the disciples (indeed, the documents show them to have acted with exemplary normality--as typically sinful and insensitive members of a fallen race). But these same primary documents do force us to a miraculous understanding of the Resurrection, since any alternative explanation runs directly counter to all primary-source facts at our disposal. The documents, in short, force us to go against biological generalizations as to corpses remaining dead, but do not require us to deviate from psychological generalizations as to individual and crowd behavior. Contrary to what Flew imagines, we do not arbitrarily prefer biological miracles over psychological miracles; we accept no miracles unless the primary evidence compels us to it, and if that evidence requires psychological miracles rather than biological ones, we would go that route.[31]

Take for example the above case of Mrs. D having been healed of her arthritis. Would it be plausible to arbitrarily assert that her healing did *not* in fact occur but that all the evidence converging upon the event for some inexplicable reason is faulty? Suppose that someone merely pontificates that the witness of the members of her congregation, her life-long pain, the repeated confirmation of her doctors' diagnosis, and her subsequent post-prayer relief, etc. were products of a giant psychological "miracle". Would such an assertion be *just as* valid as saying that a miracle actually happened? Would it explain the known facts in a simple and coherent manner? Not in the slightest. For there is nothing within the body of the evidence that calls for an interpretation of this event along these lines. It is absurd to assert without any evidence whatsoever that such an interpretation is plausible.

This is not to say that Flew does not make some valid points concerning miracles and history. For instance, I think that Flew is correct in saying that the critical historian should be skeptical when confronted with an alleged miracle. However, if the facts surrounding the event cannot be plausibly explained except by positing a miraculous interpretation, then the critical historian would be acting arbitrarily if he merely asserted that the evidence *must* be faulty (in an almost "miraculous" sense) because miracles do not happen.

Thus it is the primary-source evidence for a particular event that finally determines whether or not it actually occurred. And when interpreting this event only the evidence can serve as the data by which a proper interpretation is arrived at and also as a proper safeguard against interpretations which are foreign to the facts of the case.

Argument from Identification

In his third argument, Flew defends the assertion that a miracle, apart from some sort of rich and positive natural theology,[32] cannot be identified as having its source in the divine. Flew writes:

> Given a rich and positive natural theology the historian could perhaps find there natural means to identify overriding acts of God. He could thus distinguish what is naturally possible from what, on privileged occasions, in fact occurs. What is naturally impossible is nevertheless possible to God.[33]

But given his assumption that there is no compelling independent evidence for God's existence,[34] Flew asserts:

> We have. . . got to have, and we have got to be able to recognize by natural (as opposed to revealed) means, overridings of that natural (as opposed to Transcendent) order. The crunch comes over the problem of identification. The great temptation is to assume that we have some natural (as opposed to revealed) means of telling that something, notwithstanding that it actually did happen, nevertheless could not have happened naturally (in the other sense). We have not. Our only

way of determining the capacities and incapacities of Nature is to study what does in fact occur. Suppose, for instance, that all previous observation and experiment had suggested that some performance was beyond human power; and suppose then we find, to our amazement, that after all some people can do it. Still this by itself is a reason, not for postulating a series of infusions of supernatural grace, but for shaking up the psychological assumptions which these discoveries have discredited.[35]

He writes elsewhere:

The natural scientist, confronted with some occurrence inconsistent with a proposition previously believed to express a law of nature, can find in this disturbing inconsistency no ground whatever for proclaiming that the particular law of nature has been supernaturally overridden. . . We certainly cannot say, on any natural (as opposed to revealed) grounds, that anything that actually happens is beyond the powers of unaided nature, any more than we can say that anything any man has ever succeeded in doing transcends all merely human powers.[36]

This argument can be summarized in the following way:

1. Before one can know that a miracle has occurred, it must be able to be identified.

2. An alleged miracle can either have its source in the natural or the supernatural.

3. But if one asserts that the alleged miracle has its source in the supernatural (i.e., God), one begs the question.

4. But if one asserts that the alleged miracle has its source in the natural, it ceases to be supernatural, and is therefore not a miracle.

5. Therefore, since a miracle cannot be identified, it cannot be known to have occurred.

This argument is a sophisticated defense of Hume's assertion "That a miracle can never be proved, so as to be the foundation of a system of religion."[37] Essentially Flew is asserting that just because an event is highly unusual in terms of our knowledge of nature, this does not mean that God was responsible for the event; after all, how do we know whether or not God exists?

In response to this argument, several points should be made. For instance, we have already seen (in chapter 5) that the evidentialist (Flew is one of them) is wrong in claiming that the theist, in order to be rational, must produce evidence for God's existence. Furthermore, we have seen (in chapter 5) that it is possible to argue convincingly from the regularities found in the *natural* world that there exists an ontological ground *beyond* it, namely, a personal Creator of everything that is. It is interesting to note that Flew does not address this sort of cosmological argument, but settles for presenting the usual garden-variety objections to the Thomistic and Leibnizian arguments.[38] Therefore, since the theist is rational in believing that there exists a rational being *beyond* the natural, he is not begging the question when he asserts that there exists a supernatural being who can be responsible for miracles.

However, the question remains as to whether it is possible for the believer in miracles to make an epistemological distinction between an event in the natural world that is naturally caused and an event in the natural world that is supernaturally caused. Although we anticipated this sort of question in our analysis of Hume's argument, a summary of our conclusions, in light of Flew's objections, is needed.

We have already seen that it is perfectly coherent to speak of a violation of natural law (see chapters 2 and 3). A violation can be defined as an event which is rationally inexplicable under current scientific law and there is no new law under which it can be subsumed, and because it is a non-recurring anomaly it is highly doubtful whether it would ever be explicable in terms of any forthcoming scientific law.

We are arguing that given the fact that an event is a violation of natural law, and hence is not part of a recurring pattern of events (either anomalous or lawful), and because it occurs within a particular religious and historical context at a particular time, meaning and purpose is attached to it; that is, based on the analogy of our own experience, we infer from the convergence of these events that a certain message is being conveyed by a rational being who has the ability to control nature. Given these facts, the believer is within his epistemic rights to assert that this event was caused by a rational being outside the normal recurring pattern of events.

In light of the above and what we have covered in detail elsewhere, consider the following example we employed in chapter 4. Suppose that a purported miracle-worker, C, says that he is God's chosen and that he will perform a miracle, R, a resurrection, at time *t* in order to confirm God's approval on his mission. Furthermore, C is vehemently opposed by the religious elite who insist that he is *not* God's chosen. Moreover, every person who has ever made similar claims has remained dead (and this also goes for those who will make these claims afterwards). Therefore, if C performs R at time *t*, it seems entirely reasonable to believe that C is God's chosen one. Given its human impossibility, its uniqueness, the reasonableness in believing in God's existence, C's claim that God is responsible for R, its existential and teleological significance (i.e., C performed R at a particular time *t*, not at any other time), and the religious context of the event (i.e., C performed R when his claims about himself hinged on the actuality of R occurring at time *t*), it becomes apparent that a particular message is being communicated through this event, namely, *C is God's chosen one.*

As I noted in chapter 4, many of the miracles found in the Bible seem to be inexplicable apart from inferring a non-natural rational cause. One example is Moses' ability to split the Red Sea by vocal command in order to successfully complete the escape of the Israelites from Egypt (Exodus 14). Another one is Elijah's calling down of fire from heaven at Mt. Carmel in order to convince his pagan adversaries of the reality and superiority of Jehovah (I Kings 18).

Hence, for the believer in miracles, a miraculous event can be identified as an event which is (1) scientifically inexplicable in terms of natural law, (2) occurs within a significant historical and religious context, and (3) is performed by a God. We infer (3) from the message being communicated by the convergence of particular facts upon the event, in addition to the reasonableness of believing that such a being exists on independent grounds. This is not to say that this judgment is incorrigible. On the contrary, like all empirical judgments, a judgment concerning the occurrence of a miracle may have to be altered or discarded altogether in light of new facts and findings. Nevertheless, the fact remains that Flew is incorrect when he says that the theist is incapable of identifying the miraculous.

However, what if we view Flew's argument as making the stronger claim that it is perfectly alright, regardless of the evidence, to *always* say that *everything* that occurs in nature is ultimately natural? He seems to be saying this when he asserts that "we certainly cannot say, on any natural (as opposed to revealed) grounds, that anything that actually happens is beyond the powers of unaided nature."[39] He writes elsewhere that "if something occurs inconsistent with some proposition previously believed to express such a law, this occurrence is, not an occasion for proclaiming a miraculous violation, but a reason for confessing the error of the former belief, and for resolving to search for the law which does hold."[40] Since this view so closely resembles McKinnon's argument, we will deal with it below in our analysis of McKinnon's anti-supernaturalism.

ALASTAIR MCKINNON'S ANTI-SUPERNATURALISM

In objecting to the miraculous, McKinnon claims that any alleged miracle can be reduced to a natural event. He writes that it is "the scientist's resolve to treat all events as subject to natural law."[41]

Explaining this position, he continues:

> This does not mean that he [the scientist] insists that events should conform to some conception he already has. Nor does it mean that he disregards those which he has not yet been able to fit within such a conception. Rather, it means that he has resolved to view all events in this light. For him, *law* is a slogan; it is the way in which he proposes to look at the world. His acceptance of all events as expressions of natural law is the way in which he guides himself in his attempt to discover the real content of this conception. It is therefore essential that he refuse to treat any event as discrepant. This is not to say that certain scientists have not so treated events upon convenient occasion. It is only to say that when they have done so they have ceased to be scientists.[42]

He writes elsewhere:

> The idea of a suspension of natural law is self- contradictory. . . The contradiction may stand out more clearly if for natural law we substitute the expression *the actual course of events*. *Miracle* would then be defined as "an event involving the suspension of the actual course of events". And someone who insisted on describing an event as a miracle would be in the rather odd position of claiming that its occurrence was contrary to the actual course of events.[43]

McKinnon's argument can be put in the following way:

1. A natural event is one which occurs in the actual course of events.

2. A miracle, which is alleged to be actual, is defined as an event that violates the actual course of events.

3. But that which is actual, is actual, and is therefore by definition part of the actual course of events.

4. Therefore, belief in miracles is unreasonable.

When McKinnon's "good scientist" examines an alleged miraculous event, he relegates that event to the realm of "coincidence" or "inexplicable anomaly," with the thought in mind that it is ultimately explicable within the natural order of things.[44]

In this book a miracle has been defined as an event, because of its law-violating nature and its religious and historical context, that seems inexplicable apart from any divine intervention (see chapter 2). McKinnon, along with Flew, challenges this identification on the grounds that all "miracles," because they occur in the natural world, must be explained in terms of a wholly naturalistic world-view. In other words, because of his belief that the concept of miracle involves a contradiction, McKinnon assumes that no event in the natural world could reasonably attributed to a supernatural cause.

The first two premises of McKinnon's argument can be easily accepted by the believer in miracles: (1) A natural event is one which occurs in the natural course of events; and (2) A miracle, which is alleged to be actual, is defined as an event that violates the actual course of events. However, it is the third premise which is our chief concern: But that which is actual, is actual, and is therefore by definition part of the actual course of events. There is at least one problem with this premise. McKinnon makes the assumption that because all events that actually occur happen in the natural world, therefore all events that happen in the natural world have *ipso facto* natural causes. This is an example of the fallacy of undistributed middle.[45] This fallacy occurs when a term found in each premise of a syllogism is not properly distributed. For example:

(1) Elephants have *big ears*.

Socrates has *big ears*.

Therefore, Socrates is an elephant.

The middle term in this argument, *big ears*, is not properly distributed in all the premises, and for this reason, this argument is invalid. In order for *big ears* to be properly distributed, the first premise would have to state that *only* elephants have big ears. Example:

(2) *Only* elephants have big ears.

Socrates has big ears.

Therefore, Socrates is an elephant.

The term "only" in the first premise of (2) universalizes the middle term and therefore makes the argument formally valid. However, despite its validity, (2) is an *unsound* argument, because it is simply not true that *only elephants have big ears.* Returning to the third premise of McKinnon's argument, we can put in the form of a syllogism:

(3) Natural events occur in the natural world.

Miracles occur in the natural world.

Therefore, miracles are nothing but natural events.

The middle term in this argument, *occur in the natural world*, is not properly distributed. This argument is fallacious because it does not logically follow that miracles are naturally caused just because miracles and natural events have in common the middle term that they occur in the natural world. Hence, this argument commits the fallacy of undistributed middle. In the same way, (1) is fallacious because it does not logically follow that because Socrates and elephants both have big ears Socrates is therefore an elephant. To make (3) formally valid, McKinnon could argue:

(4) *Only* natural events happen in the natural world.

Miracles occur in the natural world.

Therefore, miracles are nothing but natural events.

Even though (4) is formally valid, it is unsound because, like (2), its first premise is dubitable. After all, the very point that McKinnon (also Flew) is trying to prove is that miracles are nothing but natural events (or should be treated as such). Therefore, to assume the first premise that only natural events happen in the natural world is to beg the question.

No matter which way he goes, McKinnon is shut down. If he opts for (3), he ends up with an invalid argument, and if he opts for validity, he ends up with an unsound argument which begs the question. Thus "the *actual* is not automatically the *natural*. What actually occurs may just as well be a supernatural event. What the naturalist must do in order to prove that an actual event is a natural event is to show that the event is naturally connected with antecedent and consequent events."[46]

Since we have already seen that natural law and a violation of natural law are logically compatible concepts (see chapters 2 and 3), McKinnon's contention that "the idea of a suspension of natural law is self-contradictory" does not have to be accepted. Furthermore, McKinnon and Flew do not take seriously their own notions of "rationality" and "nature" when they claim that we have no natural grounds by which to assert what is and is not beyond the scope of nature's capacities. For example, Flew, in a critical piece on the irrationality of theistic belief, writes:

Now to assert that such and such is the case is necessarily equivalent to deny that such and such is not the case. . . For if the utterance is indeed an assertion, it will necessarily be equivalent to a denial of the negation of that assertion. And anything which would count against the assertion, or which would induce the speaker to withdraw it and to admit that it had been mistaken, must be part of (or the whole of) the meaning of the negation of that assertion. . . And if there is nothing which a putative assertion denies then there is nothing which it asserts either: and so it is not really an assertion.[47]

Hence, if the rationality of an assertion is contingent upon some contrary state of affairs as being possible, then to simply say that the scientist should treat an alleged miraculous event as a mere scientific oddity *ad infinitum* is to be guilty of special pleading and irrationality. Moreover, if the "natural" is compatible with everything and anything that may occur in the natural world, the term "natural" has lost any significant meaning. This is not to say that we should resort to the interpretation of miracle whenever an anomalous event occurs. Rather, we are asserting that the non-theist should take seriously the strength of well-established natural law, especially if science's problem-solving capacity has been completely impotent in explaining an alleged miracle in terms of any known law (and is not even remotely close in a forthcoming explanation), as in the case of the primary law-violating miracles of the Christian tradition (e.g., resurrections, changing water into wine, walking through walls, levitating, multiplying fishes and loaves, instantaneously healing lepers, walking on water, etc.). Although it is certainly *possible* that scientific explanations of these events will someday be discovered, the fact that the possibility is currently remote, and that science has been incapable of finding *any* explanations, should count for something. Hence, we do have natural, albeit corrigible, grounds by which to assert what is and is not beyond the scope of nature's capacities.[48] Therefore, if a true non-recurring violation of a well-established natural law occurs within a particular religious and historical context, and its actuality and timing appear to convey a message, the believer in miracles is within his epistemic rights to assert that this event was caused by a rational being outside the normal course of nature.

This is not to say that McKinnon and Flew are not free to call alleged miraculous events "natural" if they so choose. After all, the nature of empirical judgments, unlike the tautological judgments of mathematics, are such that there are always other *logically* possible explanations. However, what is logically possible is not always what is rationally warranted by the evidence.

PATRICK NOWELL-SMITH'S CASE AGAINST MIRACLES

Nowell-Smith's essay against the miraculous is another variation on

Hume's assertion that "a miracle can never be proved, so as to be the foundation of a system of religion."[49] Nowell-Smith argues that the explanation which makes an event miraculous--that it is an intervention by God into the normal course of nature--is really no explanation at all. I believe that one can find at least two arguments against the miraculous in Nowell-Smith's essay.[50]

Argument From Supernatural Agency

Nowell-Smith asserts that just because an anomaly occurs in nature (as in the case of many alleged miracles, such as resurrections) does not mean that one must necessarily postulate a rational agent (God) to account for it. As he writes, "If any scientist has said that a certain phenomena 'is inexplicable as the effect of natural agents and *therefore* be ascribed to supernatural agents', he is not speaking as a scientist, but as a philosopher." In other words, "no matter how strange an event someone reports, the statement that it must have been due to a supernatural agent cannot be part of that report."[51]

Since this argument overlaps much of what was presented by Flew and McKinnon, the following comments should suffice. The believer in miracles agrees with Nowell-Smith that an anomaly in itself is an insufficient reason to postulate a rational agent (God) to explain an event, especially when the anomaly is a recurring one, as in the case of Newton's observation of the perturbed orbits of the planets. However, when the believer in miracles states that an anomalous event is miraculous he is saying that the event is uniquely anomalous (non-recurring) and occurs within a significant religious and historical context, and thus conveys a meaning and message which is best explained by postulating a rational agent. That is, the strangeness of the event itself is not the sole reason the theist postulates a rational agent; other factors have definite bearing on his judgment.

Nowell-Smith asserts that if a scientist postulates a rational agent, he is no longer acting as a scientist but as a philosopher. That this may be the case matters little for the plausibility of the claimed postulate. For it is certainly possible that this postulate is entirely plausible while not being strictly "scientific" as Nowell-Smith defines this term. After all, there are all sorts of "truths" that are strictly non-scientific but nevertheless reasonable to believe. For example, the moral, methodological, and epistemic values of science itself are assumed but are not scientifically demonstrable; these values are *philosophical*, not scientific.[52] In addition, historical, legal, and behavioral explanations, although falling outside the strict rubric of science, can nevertheless be plausible and reasonable to believe (and oftentimes include rational agents in their explanations). Hence if the method of science prevents one from postulating a unique rational agent in order to explain the occurrence of an event when such a postulate is made plausible by the facts, so much the worse for the method of science.

Argument from Scientific Explanation

Nowell-Smith's second argument, which really underlies what he argues for in his first, asserts that only that which is lawfully predictable in terms of science is able to truly explain an event. And since a miracle is incapable of being lawfully predicted, a miracle cannot serve as an explanation of an anomalous event. Nowell-Smith writes that "a scientific explanation is an hypothesis from which prediction can be made, which can afterwards be verified. It is of the essence of such an hypothesis--a 'law' is but a well-confirmed hypothesis--that it should be capable of such predictive expansion." Hence, the supernaturalist's "explanations are inevitably *ex post facto*; we can only recognize a miracle after it has occurred."[53] According to Nowell-Smith, inevitably these anomalies will be explicable in terms of scientific law. The following is an outline of this argument:

1. All explanations must be lawful.

2. A miracle is an explanation of an event.

3. With laws one is able to predict the events these laws are supposed to explain.

4. Since one cannot predict a miracle, miracle is inadequate to function as an explanation of an event.

In response to this argument, several comments are in order. First, J.P. Moreland points out that "the statement 'only what can be known by science or quantified and empirically tested is rational and true' is self-refuting."[54] He goes on to say:

> This statement itself is not a statement *of* science. It is a philosophical statement *about* science. How could the statement itself be quantified and empirically tested? And if it cannot, then by the statement's own standards, it cannot itself be true or rationally held.[55]

Therefore, as we noted earlier, it is plain that there are other sorts of explanations and truths which are outside the realm of lawfully predictable science.

Second, Paul J. Dietl has made the observation that many miracle-claims were *predicted* prior to their occurrence, but "were not made possible by anything Nowell-Smith would call a law." For example, "a prediction was involved in the Elijah story," however, "that the prediction did not rest on knowledge of a regularity between initial conditions and effect was the reason for looking to the supernatural." As he puts it: ". . . I do not see how one could pin down God as the independent variable unless predictions like those were possible."[56]

Third, there are explanations, especially those employed in the analysis of human intentions, which are not scientifically lawful as Nowell-Smith defines it. For example, suppose we ask James, a person who frequents Sam's Town Race and Sports Book, "Why did you choose to put your money on the Lakers when you knew that their best players were injured?" Now he may respond, "I had some inside information, which I thought was accurate, which led me to believe that those players were healthy." Now this sort of explanation is not scientifically lawful yet perfectly acceptable. It is also *ex post facto*; that is, unpredictable in terms of any law (e.g., All J's bet on L's at time *t*) yet explanatory after the fact.

And it should be kept in mind that when the theist says that a miracle is an explanation of a violation of natural law, he is saying that it was brought about by the intention of a rational agent, a god. Therefore, since it is not necessary that intentionality be capable of being predicted on the basis of a particular scientific law in order to be a plausible explanation for an event, miracle as explanation is perfectly acceptable even though it is not predictable in terms of scientific law. As Dietl comments:

> This is all the more pressing since part of the point of interpreting an event as a miracle is to see it not as a natural event but as an action, or result of an action, of an intelligent being. That all intelligible *actions* are subsumable under laws is even less credible than that all *events* are. An action can be made intelligible by showing its *point* (for example, to bring wayward children back to the truth, to reward the holy, to save the chosen people, etc.), and showing the good of an action is not automatically to subsume it under a law.[57]

Even if human intentions could be predictable in terms of some yet unknown laws, this would not take away from our argument. After all, we are arguing that in our *current* state of knowledge, *ex post facto* explanations of human intentions are perfectly acceptable even when there are no definite scientifically predictable laws under which they can be subsumed. Furthermore, although the results of human intentions are oftentimes subsumable under some scientific laws, the intentions themselves are not lawful in any real scientific sense. For example, Patrick throwing Lizzie the football conforms to the laws of mechanics, but there is no law to explain the throwing of the football in terms of Patrick's intention to throw it in the direction of Lizzie. Drawing an analogy with a miraculous explanation, one may be able to "see" the intervention of a rational agent in an anomalous event only after one reflects on certain aspects of the event that may lead one to infer this conclusion, just as one can know that Patrick's intention was to throw the football at Lizzie only after the event has occurred (or if he tells you beforehand, as in the case of "predictive" miracles such as Elijah's).

Of course, the case for rational intervention, and hence intentionality, in an anomalous event is bolstered if the miracle-worker who claims a god's allegiance is able to reproduce miraculous events at the calling of a god's name. In fact, denial of rational intervention at this point becomes highly irrational. Although I do not necessarily agree with all his comments, Tan Tai Wei cites the miracles of Jesus' ministry as an example:

> Assume, say that Jesus had really predicted his own death and resurrection, claimed his miraculous feats to be deliberate so as to demonstrate his 'Sonship' to the 'Father', and that we have empirical certainty that there were a few occasions at least where such exceptional phenomena occurred in strict coincidence with such demonstrations of his divinity. Now, one such occurrence, although enough to generate wonder, might be reasonably presumed after deliberation to be an accidentally coinciding natural phenomenon. Such a conclusion, though, would already seem unduly sceptical if, say, the raising of Lazarus was the only miracle of Jesus. For Jesus had confidently ordered the removal of the grave stone, prayed aloud that God should there prove his power, and then cried 'Lazarus, come forth!' And he did. And if such feats had indeed been so frequent as to be common in the life of such a person, then even if it be conceded that the exceptions, though unrepeatable or rarely repeatable, are nevertheless merely natural phenomena, the question still left unanswered is why the repeated coincidence of such rarity within the intentions and performances of this one man obtains. . . At some point, abandoning scepticism would be more rational, because here some of our ordinary criteria (which are independent of religious considerations), governing the rational acceptability of purported coincidences as merely natural ones, would not be met.[58]

Finally, to suppose, as Nowell-Smith does, that science will inevitably find natural explanations for alleged miraculous events is special pleading. Furthermore, it does not take into consideration the failure of science in explaining (and the extremely remote future possibility of doing so) the primary law-violating miracles of the Christian tradition. Moreover, Nowell-Smith's assertion is a faith proposition, which is highly unscientific by his own standards, and somewhat religious. And as in the case of Flew and McKinnon, Nowell-Smith does not take seriously what we ordinarily mean by "natural law" and "rationality".

NOTES FOR CHAPTER SIX

[1]For a detailed historical summary of the debate after Hume, see Colin Brown *Miracles and the Critical Mind* (Grand Rapids, MI: Eerdmans, 1984), pp. 103-277.

[2]For example, Antony Flew, "Miracles," in *Encyclopedia of Philosophy*, vol. 5, ed. Paul Edwards (New York: Macmillan & The Free Press, 1967), pp. 346-353; Antony Flew, "Parapsychology Revisited: Laws, Miracles, and Repeatability," in *Philosophy and Parapsychology*, ed. Jan Ludwig (Buffalo, NY: Prometheus Books, 1978), pp. 263-269; Antony Flew, *God: A Critical Enquiry*, 2nd ed.(LaSalle, IL: Open Court, 1984); Antony Flew, "The Impossibility of the Miraculous," in *Hume's Philosophy of Religion*, the Sixth James Montgomery Hester Seminar (Winston-Salem, NC: Wake Forest University Press, 1986), pp. 9-32; and Antony Flew in *Did Jesus Rise From the Dead?: The Resurrection Debate*, ed. Terry L. Miethe (New York: Harper & Row, 1987)

[3]Stephen T. Davis also claims that Flew offers three arguments, although Davis' interpretation of these arguments is slightly different from mine. See Stephen T. Davis, "Is it Possible to Know that Jesus was Raised from the Dead?" *Faith and Philosophy*, 2 (April 1984): 149-150. Furthermore, there could be a possible fourth argument (see Flew, "Parapsychology Revisited"), but because I believe it underlies his first argument and is nearly identical to Nowell-Smith's position against the miraculous (both of which will be critiqued), I have chosen not to deal with it as a seperate Flewian argument.

[4]Flew, *God: A Critical Enquiry*, p. 140.

[5]*Ibid.*

[6]Flew, "Miracles," p. 352.

[7]For example, as we noted in detail elsewhere (see notes for chapter 3), "legal science, as an outgrowth of millennia of court decisions, developed meticulous criteria for distinguishing factual truth from error." John Warwick Montgomery, *The Law Above the Law* [Minneapolis: Dimension Books, 1975], p. 86).

[8]Flew, "Miracles," p. 352.

[9]R.F. Holland uses the term "conceptually impossible." He writes that "a miracle, though it cannot only be this, must at least be something the occurrence of which can be categorized at one and the same time as empirically certain and conceptually impossible." (R.F. Holland, "The

Miraculous," in *Logical Analysis and Contemporary Theism*, ed. John Donnelly [New York: Fordham University Press, 1972], p. 232).

10William Lane Craig, *Apologetics: An Introduction* (Chicago: Moody, 1984), p. 123.

11*Ibid.*

12Flew, *God: A Critical Enquiry*, p. 140. Hume's original citation is found in an additional note to his *An Enquiry Concerning Human Understanding*, 3rd edition, text revised and notes P.H. Nidditch, intro. and analytic index L.A. Selby-Bigge (Oxford: Clarendon, 1975; reprinted from the 1777 edition), p. 345.

13As quoted in Flew, *Ibid.*

14Davis, "Is it Possible," p. 149. John Warwick Montgomery interprets Flew's argument in a similar way. See his, "Science, Theology, and the Miraculous," in his *Faith Founded on Fact* (New York: Thomas Nelson, 1978), pp. 52-58.

15Davis, "Is it Possible," p. 150.

16This is Davis' point when he writes: "Why cannot nature, so to speak, almost but not quite always act regularly and (if we knew enough) predictably? If it does, then those who wish to argue for certain irregularities will naturally do so on the basis of regularities seen elsewhere. If there do turn out to be unique events, not analogous to any others (and some scientists argue that there are such events, e.g. the 'big bang'), we will have no choice but to try to argue for them on the basis of regular and repeatable events." (*Ibid.*) For a fuller presentation of how singularities can be known on the basis of regularities, see chapter 4.

17Montgomery, "Science," p. 56.

18*Ibid.*, p. 54.

19Flew, "Miracles," p. 352.

20We know this to be the case because of what Flew writes directly following the above quote: "If one once departs in such arbitrary ways from these canons of critical history, then anything and everything goes. (For examples of precisely this sort of arbitrariness, see M.C. Perry, *The Easter Enigma*, London and New York, 1959.)" (*Ibid*). See also, Flew, *God: A Critical Inquiry*, pp. 149-150.

[21]That is, these appearances were really the foundation of the disciples' belief, *not* the empty tomb. On the historicity of these appearances, New Testament scholar Norman Perrin writes: "The more we study the tradition with regard to the appearances, the firmer the rock begins to appear upon which they are based." (Norman Perrin, *The Resurrection According to Matthew, Mark, and Luke* [Philadelphia: Fortress, 1977], p. 80) See also, John Aslup, *The Post-Resurrection Appearances of the Gospel Tradition* (Stuttgart: Calwer Verlag, 1975); and C.H. Dodd, "The Appearances of the Risen Christ: An Essay in Form-Criticism of the Gospels," in *More New Testament Studies* (Manchester: University of Manchester, 1968), pp. 102-133.

[22]Montgomery, "Science," pp. 54.

[23]*Ibid.*, pp. 54-55.

[24]Antony Flew, "Theology and Falsification," in *New Essays in Philosophical Theology*, ed. Antony Flew and Alasdair MacIntyre (New York: Macmillan, 1955), pp. 98-99.
    Probably the best response to the falsification challenge is by Alvin Plantinga in his *God and Other Minds* (Ithaca, NY: Cornell University Press, 1967), pp. 156-168. See also, Stephen T. Davis, *Faith, Skepticism, and Evidence: An Essay in Religious Epistemology* (Cranbury, NJ: Associated University Presses, 1978), pp. 191-213.

[25]Flew, "Theology and Falsification," p. 107.

[26]In a 1985 debate (published in book form in 1987) with Gary R. Habermas, Flew does not seem to have altered this earlier view concerning miracles when he states: "I have tried to show that and to explain why purely historical evidence *cannot* establish the occurrence of any authentic miracle, not, that is, until and unless those presuppositions can be corrected and supplemented, either by a rich and relevant antecedent revelation or by a rich and relevant natural theology" (my emphasis). (Flew in *Did Jesus Rise From the Dead?*, p. 7).

[27]Flew questions the strength of such an apologetic when he writes: "It is simply not taking the task of historical investigation seriously to assume that the sole alternative to accepting this miracle must be to suggest 'that men would first concoct a lie and then proceed to die for their faith in it'. . ." (Flew, *God: A Critical Enquiry*, p. 152).
    On the contrary, this sort of objection does not take the historical nature of the Christian faith seriously. The classic apologetic does not rest solely on the disciples' inability to die for a self-perpetuated lie, but is a cumulative case of convergent facts: the historicity of the empty tomb and post-resurrection appearances, the inability of *all* the

disciples to be deceived, the inadequacy of naturalistic theories to explain the Resurrection, *and* the martyrdom of the disciples. See Gary R. Habermas, *The Resurrection of Jesus* (Lanham, MD: University Press of America, 1980)

[28]Gary R. Habermas in *Did Jesus Rise from the Dead?*, p. 25. Few, if any scholars, dispute these facts. Take for example the following *critical* scholars who accept the historicity of these facts: Rudolf Bultmann, *Theology of the New Testament*, trans. Kendrick Grobel, 2 vols. (New York: Charles Scribner's Sons, 1951, 1955), 1: 44-55; Paul Tillich, *Systematic Theology*, 3 vols. (Chicago: University of Chicago Press, 1951, 1957, 1963), 2: 153-158; Gunther Bornkamm, *Jesus of Nazareth*, trans. Irene and Fraser McLuskey with James M. Robinson (New York: Harper and Row, 1960), pp. 179-186; Reginald H. Fuller, *Formation of the Resurrection Narratives* (New York: Macmillan, 1971), pp. 27-49; Ulrich Wilckens, *Resurrection*. trans. A.M. Stewart (Edinburgh, Scotland: Saint Andrews Press, 1977), pp. 112-113; Wolfhart Pannenberg, *Jesus--God and Man*, trans. L.L. Wilkens and D. Priebe (Philadelphia: Westminster, 1968), pp. 88-106; Raymond Brown, *The Virginal Conception and Bodily Resurrection of Jesus* (New York: Paulist Press, 1973), pp. 81-92; Jurgen Moltmann, *Theology of Hope*, trans. James W. Leith (New York: Harper and Row, 1967), pp. 197-202; A.M. Hunter, *Jesus: Lord and Savior* (Grand Rapids, MI: Eerdmans, 1976), pp. 98-103; Norman Perrin, *Resurrection According to Matthew, Mark and Luke* (Philadelphia: Fortress Press, 1977), pp. 78-84; and Paul Van Buren, *The Secular Meaning of the Gospel* (New York: Macmillan, 1963), pp. 126-134.

[29]See Habermas, *The Resurrection of Jesus*, pp. 26-33; and Gary Habermas, *The Resurrection of Jesus: A Rational Inquiry* (Ann Arbor, MI: University Microfilms, 1976), pp. 114-171. Karl Barth has made the observation that critical scholars no longer give consideration to these naturalistic theories simply because these theories are inconsistent with the facts, and hence "today we rightly turn up our noses at this." (Karl Barth, *Church Dogmatics*, ed. G.W. Bromiley and T.F. Torrance, 13 vols. [Edinburgh, Scotland: T. and T. Clark, 1961], 4 [part one]: 340).

[30]See Robert H. Stein, "Was the Tomb Really Empty?" *Journal of the Evangelical Theological Society*, 20 (March 1977): 23-29. Concerning the empty tomb, Pannenberg has observed that the early Jewish polemic against Christianity presupposed the reality of the empty tomb (albeit with a quite different interpretation of its vacancy), and that this fact is "among the general historical arguments that speak for the trustworthiness of the report about the discovery of Jesus' empty tomb." (Pannenberg, *Jesus*, p. 101). See also, Michael Grant, *Jesus: An Historian's Review of the Gospels* (New York: Charles Scribner's Sons, 1977), p. 176.

31Montgomery, "Science," p. 57.

32In his debate with Habermas, it seems that Flew has recently modified this position:
"HABERMAS: . . . Let's introduce a hypothetical situation here. A naturalist is arguing with a theist about the Resurrection, and the theist pushes the naturalist and the naturalist comes to admit that, indeed, the Resurrection is a historical event. At that point, would the naturalist have to be at least open to the theist's claim that Jesus is deity and that he speaks authoritatively from God?"
FLEW: Yes, that seems to be clear." (Flew and Habermas in *Did Jesus Rise From the Dead?*, p. 49).

33Flew, *God: A Critical Enquiry*, p. 146.

34*Ibid.*, pp. 52-117

35*Ibid.*, p. 143.

36Flew, "Miracles," p. 349.

37Hume, *Enquiry*, p. 127.

38Flew, *God: A Critical Enquiry*, pp. 69-92. For responses to Flewian-type objections to these arguments, see Norman L. Geisler and Winfried Corduan "The Cosmological Argument Reevaluated," chapter 9 of their *Philosophy of Religion*, 2nd ed. (Grand Rapids, MI: Baker Book House, 1988), pp. 175-207, and William L. Rowe, "Two Criticisms of the Cosmological Argument," in *Logical Analysis and Contemporary Theism*, pp. 20-40.

39Flew, "Miracles," p. 349.

40Flew, *God: A Critical Enquiry*, p. 114.

41Alastair McKinnon, "'Miracle' and 'Paradox'," *American Philosophical Quarterly*, 4 (October 1967): 314.

42*Ibid.*

43*Ibid.*, p. 309.

44Gary Gutting takes a similar stance when he writes: "It is sometimes said that miracle in this sense would have to be a 'violation of the laws of nature'; that is, the occurrence of an event inconsistent with some true causal generalization about the world. If so, then argument from miracles is on very shaky ground, because. . . laws of nature will be consistent with any observable course of nature. Finding out that one had been violated would require establishing there were no factors (not even ones entirely unknown to present science) affecting the way the events governed by the law developed. But if the existence of such factors were excluded, surely it would be at least as reasonable to suppose that the purported law of nature was erroneous as it would be to suppose that a true law of nature had been violated by a divine action." (Gary Gutting, *Religious Belief and Religious Skepticism* [Notre Dame, IN: University of Notre Dame Press, 1982], p. 69)

[45]See Antony Flew, *Thinking Straight* (Buffalo, NY: Prometheus Books, 1975), p. 25.
  I have made the observation that the objection to contemporary rock music on the part of some members of the clergy commits the fallacy of undistributed middle. See Francis J. Beckwith, "Fallacy of Undistributed Middle," Bias Eq Column, *Cornerstone*, 14 (Issue 77, 1986): 42.

[46]Norman L. Geisler, *Christian Apologetics* (Grand Rapids, MI: Baker Book House, 1976), pp. 274-275.

[47]Flew, "Theology and Falsification," p. 98.

[48]Craig has made the observation that two of Flew's arguments are incompatible with each other: ". . . he asserted [in his third argument] that our knowledge of nature is so incomplete that we can never regard any event as miraculous, since it could conform to an unknown law of nature. . . [In his first argument] he asserts precisely the opposite, namely, that our knowledge of natural law is so complete that not only can we determine which events are nomologically impossible, but we are also able to impose this standard over the past to expunge such events from the record. These two positions are incompatible." (Craig, *Apologetics*, p. 123).

[49]Hume, *Enquiry*, p. 127.

[50]Patrick Nowell-Smith, "Miracles," in *New Essays*, pp. 243-253. On page 245 Nowell-Smith puts forth a "third" argument, which is practically identical to Hume's fourth criterion of Part II of his argument against miracles. We have dealt with this argument in detail elsewhere (see chapter 4).

[51]*Ibid.*, pp. 245-246.

[52]For example, see Larry Laudan, *Science and Values* (Berkeley, CA: University of California Press, 1984), and Hilary Putnam, *Reason, Truth,*

and History (New York: Cambridge University Press, 1981), pp. 132-135.

[53]Nowell-Smith, "Miracles," pp. 249-250.

[54]J.P. Moreland, *Scaling the Secular City* (Grand Rapids, MI: Baker Book House, 1987), p. 197.

[55]*Ibid.*

[56]Paul J. Dietl, "On Miracles," in *Logical Analysis and Contemporary Theism*, p. 244.

[57]*Ibid.* For a further elaboration of the difference between *scientific* and *personal* explanations, see Richard Taylor, "Two Kinds of Explanation," in *Miracles*, ed. Richard Swinburne (New York: Macmillan, 1989), pp. 103-113.

[58]Tan Tai Wei, "Recent Discussions on Miracles," *Sophia (Australia)*, 11 (October 1972): 24.

CHAPTER SEVEN

MIRACLES AND EVIDENCE

I pointed out in the first chapter that the problem of the miraculous is essentially epistemological and that there are two epistemological questions on which the miracles debate rests: (1) Is it ever reasonable to ascribe a divine source to an anomalous event in order to identify it as miraculous?; and (2) What theoretically entails sufficient evidence that a miracle has actually taken place. I believe that we adequately responded to the former question in chapters 4 and 5 when we examined part four of Hume's four-part historical criteria. In this chapter I will make some suggestions as to a possible way to answer the latter.

THE PROBLEM OF EVIDENCE

The acquisition, interpretation, and analysis of data, by which we make judgments concerning its value as evidence, is part and parcel of how we function in the world. I noted in chapter 3 that the criteria by which we judge data are based on regularities of our experience. For example, the archaeologist who discovers a papyrus with seemingly ordered markings, infers that this item is the product of human intelligence. This is because it has always been the case that papyri of this sort have been products of human intelligence. Furthermore, other regularities give the archaeologist a basis by which to employ other evidential criteria. For instance, he goes on to infer, based on what he knows about history, language, and ethnic distinctives, that the author of this papyrus was from a particular country and penned this document during a particular historical era in a certain city. The archaeologist's hypothesis concerning the origin of this document must be internally coherent and consistent with other known facts. Although his criteria are corrigible, the archaeologist knows that they have been refined by practical application, regularities of human experience, and scientific testing (such as in the case of carbon dating).

When it comes to the alleged evidence for miracle-claims, there seems to be no universally accepted criteria by which to evaluate these claims. This is mainly because most of the objections to the miraculous are pre-evidential. That is, they do not examine the evidence for particular miracles *per se*, but dispense with miracles in general prior to the examination of the evidence. As we have seen, the main reason for this is because the arguments against the miraculous usually point to the antecedent improbability of a miracle as *ipso facto* reason not to examine any evidence from the outset. In other words, no evidence is ever sufficient to make plausible the belief that a miracle has occurred.

Without repeating our critique of this sort of reasoning (see chapter 3), we concluded that just as our formulations of natural laws are based on certain regularities--which make miracles antecedently improbable because they are defined as violations of natural law--our standards of evaluating testimony and evidence are also based on certain regularities, e.g., "Witnesses in such-and-such a situation are more apt to tell the truth." Because these standards do not have the same individual probative strength as a natural law, a single piece of testimonial evidence for a miracle is not able to warrant our belief that a violation of natural law has occurred. However, if the testimonial evidence is multiplied and reinforced by circumstantial considerations (that is, other independent probabilities), and the explanation of the event as a miracle connects the data in a simple and coherent fashion, and a denial of the event's occurrence becomes an *ad hoc* naturalism-of-the-gaps, then I do not see why it would not be entirely reasonable to believe that a miracle has occurred. For its plausibility is based on a convergence of independent probabilities which is able to "outweigh" the antecedent improbability of the event occurring. This is the reason why in some unusual circumstances it is reasonable to believe that a highly improbable event has occurred.

LEGAL REASONING AND MIRACLES

I believe that the legal model of evaluating evidence should be employed in judging whether or not it is reasonable to believe that a particular miracle has taken place. My reason for this is two-fold. First, because of its practical application, "legal science, as an outgrowth of millennia of court decisions, developed meticulous criteria for distinguishing factual truth from error."[1] Hence, as a basis for evaluating evidence, it is of the highest order. Secondly, there are many similarities between miracle-claims and evidential claims involved in legal disputes. For instance, consider the following three points. (1) Miracle-claims almost always are claims attested to by witnesses. Legal reasoning involves the judging of the credibility of witnesses, and how their testimony fits in with known facts surrounding the case. (2) From this first point it follows that miracle-claims are allegedly based on evidence other than testimonial. For example, certain facts if true, such as in the case of a miraculous healing (i.e., A had rheumatoid arthritis at time t, and ceased to have this ailment at time t_2), could help to substantiate the testimony of the actuality of this occurrence. Legal reasoning involves the accessibility and the evaluating of evidence.

122

(3) Consequently, miracle-claims may involve counter-claims, that is, claims that the event did not occur. Legal reasoning involves evaluating the ability or inability of contrary evidence to disconfirm or raise doubts concerning the claim under question. This would also involve the process of cross-examination.

The reason for opting for legal reasoning instead of historical method is three-fold. First, historical method, for the most part, is employed in evaluating the evidence for historical events, yet not all miracle-claims are "historical". For instance, if a woman was allegedly healed of cancer yesterday on her death-bed, Virginia, and we want to know whether this event has occurred, historical method is of little value. Hence, legal reasoning can be used to evaluate the evidence of a greater number of alleged events than historical method. Secondly, as Russell R. Windes and Arthur Hastings have pointed out,

> Because of the fact that law deals with issues of human life and property, it has established through the years an evidential system which is rigid and inflexible, a system that imposes severe ultimate tests on the acceptability and probative value of all evidence.[2]

In other words, "evidential law imposes a rigidity seldom encountered in other disciplines."[3] Thirdly, John Warwick Montgomery has made the observation that "the advantage of a jurisprudential approach lies in the difficulty of jettisoning it: legal standards of evidence develop as essential means of resolving the most intractable disputes in society. . ."[4] Thus one cannot merely dispense with legal reasoning, on the grounds that its application may result in the plausibility of believing in the supernatural, without in turn sacrificing the evidential standards by which civilized society adjudicates life and death disputes.

The employment of legal reasoning in the evaluation of philosophical and religious questions has been encouraged by a number of contemporary philosophers. For example, Stephen Toulmin has written:

> To break the power of old models and analogies, we can provide ourselves with a new one. Logic is concerned with the soundness of the claims we make--with the solidity of the grounds we produce to support them, the firmness of the backing we provide for them--or, to change the metaphor, with the sort of *case* we present in defence of our claims. The legal analogy implied in this last way of putting the point can for once be a real help. So let us forget about psychology, sociology, technology, and mathematics, ignore the echoes of structural engineering and *collage* in the word "grounds" and "backing", and take as our model the discipline of jurisprudence. Logic (we may say) is generalised jurisprudence. Arguments can be

123

compared with law-suits, and the claims we make and argue for in extra-legal contexts with claims made in the courts, while the cases we present in making good each kind of claim can be compared with each other.[5]

In his practical logic textbook, *Critical Thinking: Consider the Verdict*, Bruce N. Waller employs the legal model in teaching critical thinking (the reader is to imagine he is on a jury weighing evidence), and draws connections "between the reasoning required in the jury box and the reasoning required in everyday situations."[6] At the conclusion of his rehabilitated version of the cosmological argument, Mortimer Adler employs legal standards when he writes that "our conclusion that God exists cannot be affirmed with certitude, but only *beyond a reasonable doubt*"[7] (my emphasis). He goes on to say:

> I am persuaded that God exists, either *beyond a reasonable doubt* or *by a preponderance of reasons* in favor of that conclusion *over reasons against it*. I am, therefore, willing to terminate this inquiry with the statement that I have *reasonable grounds* for affirming God's existence.[8] (my emphasis)

It should be noted that the use of legal reasoning in evaluating miracle-claims and supporting religious belief is nothing new. There is a long tradition in Christian apologetics of attorneys both employing legal reasoning in arguing for the historicity of Jesus' Resurrection and writing on theological topics. For instance, Hugo Grotius, known as the "father of international law," was quite possibly the first Christian apologist to put forth a well-developed historical defense for Christian theism in his *The Truth of the Christian Religion* (1627),[9] although he did not employ legal reasoning in the same rigorous way that Thomas Sherlock did in his *The Tryal of the Witnesses* (1729).[10] Most scholars believe that Hume's argument against miracles is directed against Sherlock's work.[11]

This tradition continued in the writings of Thomas Erskine, Simon Greenleaf, and Edmund H. Bennett. Erskine, who, in 1800, defended Hadfield in the classic trial for attempted regicide, authored *Remarks on the Internal Evidence for the Truth of Revealed Religion* (7th ed., 1823).[12] Greenleaf, the famous Royal Professor of Law at Harvard University, wrote *An Examination of the Testimony of the Four Evangelists by the Rules of Evidence Administered in the Courts of Justice* (1846).[13] Bennett, late dean of the Boston University School of Law, authored a book defending the internal consistency of the four Gospels, *The Four Gospels from a Lawyer's Standpoint* (1899).[14]

In the twentieth century, I.H. Linton, J.N.D. Anderson and John Warwick Montgomery are examples of thinkers who have sought to rehabilitate and refine this traditional apologetic. Linton, a member of the District of Columbia Bar and the Bar of the United States Supreme Court, is the author of *A Lawyer Examines the Bible* (1943).[15] J.N.D. Anderson, former Director of the Institute of Advanced Legal Studies in the University of London and a world-renowned expert in Muslim Law, has written three books on the topic: *A Lawyer Among the Theologians* (1973),[16] *Christianity: The Witness of History* (1969),[17] and *The Evidence for the Resurrection* (1966).[18] It is interesting to note that in a dialogue on Christ's Resurrection, liberal theologian Harvey Cox stated that he had just attended a lecture given by Anderson, which, in his opinion, was the most convincing lecture on the Resurrection he had ever heard, although for philosophical reasons (namely, resurrections are impossible) Cox still rejected the evidence.[19] An attorney and Lutheran theologian, Montgomery is probably the most qualified twentieth century Christian thinker to write on the intergration of legal reasoning and miracle-claims. He has written on this topic in numerous places.[20]

Despite this grand tradition of integrating legal reasoning and miracle-claims, little or no philosophical spadework has been done in justifying this integration. Although Montgomery responds to the contemporary philosophical objections to the miraculous,[21] he does not tell us why the evidential criteria in legal reasoning are capable of "outweighing" the antecedent improbability of the occurrence of a miracle.[22] In fact, I see this as the chief flaw in most Christian apologetic works. That is, the apologist, after showing why he believes the philosophical objections to the miraculous fail, he presents evidence for the Christian miracles, while leaving unanswered the question of why any evidence, whether it is historical or legal, can make plausible the belief that the antecedently improbable has occurred. Because the Christian apologist fails to really appreciate the force of what Hume and his contemporary defenders are saying, he has not adequately justified his course of action.[23]

I believe that in our critique of Hume's in-principle argument the necessary philosophical spadework has been completed. As we noted earlier in this chapter, we concluded that since evidential criteria themselves are based on certain probabilities (that is, regularities), it is entirely possible that one can plausibly believe that a miracle has occurred if the converging of independent probabilities (that is, the pieces of evidence) "outweighs" the antecedent improbability of the event occurring. And we know that it is reasonable to believe that this is the case if the explanation of miracle connects the data in a simple and coherent fashion, and a denial of the event's occurrence becomes an *ad hoc* naturalism-of-the-gaps.

APPLYING LEGAL REASONING

In this concluding section of this chapter, we will present a brief summary of the evidential criteria employed in legal reasoning,[24] and apply these criteria to a hypothetical case.

Windes and Hastings point out that "law is concerned with evidence in two vital areas: (1) evidence consisting of precedent growing out of former decisions rendered in courts on various civil and criminal controversies and (2) evidence in the form of proof introduced in a specific case to establish the guilt or innocence (in criminal cases) or liability or non-liability (in civil matters) of particular defendants."[25] The first type of evidence consists of the body of the law, *corpus juris*, from which courts draw general precedents which are employed in specific cases in which it is claimed that the law has been violated. For example, if an atheist organization seeks tax-exempt status as a religious organization and is denied, its attorney may take the case to court and appeal to the precedent of *Torcaso v. Watkins* (1961),[26] in which the United States Supreme Court declared that certain secular movements were "religious".

The second type of evidence "constitutes facts and opinions directly related to a present particular case under consideration by the court."[27] This is concerned with whether or not the data put forth by a plaintiff can actually support his claims about some alleged event. Because of its obvious application to the alleged evidence involved in miracle-claims, this second type of evidence will be our chief concern. According to Windes and Hastings, this type of evidence

> seeks to affirm or deny a conclusion through comment on its truth. It consists of sets of rules which are applicable to the admissibility of facts and opinions in court which seek support of an unknown disputed matter of fact. The purpose of evidence is to produce persuasion as to the truth of a conclusion.[28]

Over the centuries rules concerned with the admissibility, credibility, function, impeachment, and rehabilitation of evidence have evolved. That is, through the meticulous rigor of practical application certain criteria of evidence have been formulated. In this sense, legal reasoning is neither arbitrary nor incorrigible, but is based on the regularities of human experience. In legal reasoning, the attorney, in order to prove a particular conclusion, must demonstrate the following: "(1) that certain facts or groups of facts exist; (2) that to the contingency of their existence the state attaches the legal consequences asserted by the claimant."[29] Translating this to logical terminology, the attorney, in order to have a *sound* case, must demonstrate that his *premises* are true and that his conclusion *logically* follows from these premises.[30] John Henry Wigmore, author of a five-volume work on evidence, categorized all legal evidence in the following way:

1. The presentation of the thing itself as to which persuasion is desired, such as a weapon, broken leg, document, premises on which an act was committed, and scene of an accident. Such evidence is *presumptive* evidence, or *real*, evidence (autoptic).
2. The presentation of some independent fact by inference from which the persuasion is to be produced. This is *inferential* evidence, and consists of two forms:
   a. *Direct*, or *testimonial*, evidence--the assertion of a human being as to the existence of the thing at issue.
   b. *Indirect*, or *circumstantial*, evidence--evidence which suggests a fact at issue is true through the establishment of circumstances or facts which afford a basis for a reasonable inference of a connection between facts which are known and those that are unknown.[31]

An example of presumptive evidence would be a contract agreed upon by both plaintiff and defendant in a case in which the former is accusing the latter of breaching it. After accepting the contract as presumptive evidence, the court may decide whether or not facts have been adequately established to show beyond a reasonable doubt that the defendant had breached the contract, or, if the defendant admits to have broken it, whether or not the contract is binding. It is difficult to impeach presumptive evidence, although there may be situations in which the authenticity of such evidence is questioned (e.g., a document, weapon, etc.).[32]

On the other hand, inferential evidence is much more susceptible to impeachment. This sort of evidence involves reasoning from a particular fact or set of facts to the conclusion for which the attorney is arguing. Now this conclusion can be arrived at by actual eyewitness testimony and/or indirect (circumstantial) evidence. Thomas Starkie, in his *Evidence*, makes a distinction between these two types of inferential evidence:

Where knowledge cannot be acquired by means of actual and personal observation, there are but two modes by which the existence of a bygone fact can be ascertained: first, by information derived either immediately or mediately from those who had actual knowledge of the fact (testimonial); or secondly, by means of inferences or conclusions drawn from the facts connected with the principal fact which can be sufficiently established (circumstantial). In the first case, the inference is founded on a principle of faith, in human veracity, sanctioned by experience. In the second, the conclusion is derived by the aids of experience and reason from the connection between the facts which are known and that which is unknown.[33]

The difference between direct and indirect inferential evidence can be seen in the following example. A court may convict an accused person of embezzling money on the basis of the following direct testimonial evidence: several co-workers witnessed the accused alter financial documents, and then remove money from the company safe. Suppose, however, that the court is presented with the following indirect evidence. Several co-workers testify that the accused has bragged to them about how easy it would be to embezzle funds. One co-worker testifies that the accused purchased a new automobile (the car registration slip and proof of ownership would be presumptive evidence) which he could not possibly afford on his salary. A friend tells the court that during the past two weeks the accused was obviously disturbed about what he called his "measly salary" and angrily said that his employer is paying "slave wages". Several other co-workers testify that the accused worked on the night the money was stolen. Furthermore, a security guard testifies that he saw the accused enter and exit the building during the time the money was stolen. Although no one had actually witnessed the accused committing the robbery, on the basis of these testimonies, the court may infer that the guilt of the accused is the only plausible explanation.

Whether evidence is testimonial or indirect, the court has two basic concerns about the alleged evidence, which can be phrased in the following two questions: (1) Is the evidence relevant to the case?; and (2) Is the evidence credible? Concerning the former, the court is *not* concerned with whether or not the evidence is good or bad (that is the concern of the latter question), but whether or not the evidence is pertinent and relevant to the case. Wigmore writes:

> When the court declares testimony admissible, it declares implicitly that the sanity, experience, knowledge, etc., of the witness are such that the hypotheses of the assertion being idle chatter, ignorant gossip, or otherwise untrustworthy, are sufficiently negative *prima facie*, and that the assertion is *prima facie* worth listening to.[34]

When discussing the admissibility of evidence, "the court. . . merely inquires whether experience and precedent have sanctioned certain conditions which must accompany the evidence."[35] According to Windes and Hastings, basic to admissibility are the following three elementary criteria:

(1) The witness must know something, i.e., observed raw data.

(2) The witness must have a recollection of these observations. (3) The witness must be able and willing to accurately communicate these recollections.[36]

. After testimony is admitted by the court, its credibility comes under scrutiny. Both the expertise and the moral character of the witness are examined. Concerning the former, the court is asking whether or not the witness is qualified to testify. For example, the testimony of a doctor of forensic medicine as to the correct identification of a body is of much greater value than the testimony of an alleged relative of the deceased who claims that the body "sort of looks like him". In other words, the court considers some testimony to be of greater value than others.

The latter concerns the witness' moral qualifications. "Certain witnesses are alleged not to possess the character and reputation necessary to assure their veracity and reliability on the witness stand."[37] For example, does the witness have any vested interest in a particular outcome of the case (e.g., he stands to inherit a lot of money if the defendant is acquitted)? Is the witness so obviously biased that the veracity of his testimony can easily be questioned (e.g., there is a good indication that the witness may have such a strong personal affection for the defendant that he will do anything to prevent the defendant from going to prison)? Does the witness have a criminal record which may cause a jury to strongly doubt his reliability (e.g., he has been convicted of perjury and fraud)? Along the same lines, Patrick L. McCloskey and Ronald L. Schoenberg present a four-part test for exposing a lying witness: (1) Internal defects of the witness himself; (2) External defects of the witness himself; (3) Internal defects of the testimony itself; and (4) External defects of the testimony itself.[38]

Concerning (1), the court is inquiring as to whether the witness is a known liar (e.g., perjurer) or has a reputation for being neither trustworthy nor dependable. (2) refers to possible reasons for the witness to falsify his testimony (e.g., vested interest in the outcome).

> Not all perjurers have committed prior immoral acts or prior crimes. Frequently, law abiding citizens whose pasts are without blemish will commit perjury, not because they are inherently unworthy, but because some specific present reason compels them to do so in the case at bar. Motive, then, becomes the common denominator. There is a motive for every act of perjury. The second major way in which the cross-examiner can seek to expose perjury, therefore, is to isolate the specific motive which causes the witness to commit perjury.[39]

(3) is asking whether the witness' testimony itself is either internally inconsistent or self-contradictory. For example, if a witness

testifies at one point that he has never owned a weapon, but at another point admits to having purchased a gun registration, his testimony is inconsistent. (4) concerns how testimony squares with known facts external to the case. For example, if a witness claims that he saw the accused lifting weights at the Las Vegas Athletic Club late Saturday evening at 10 p.m., but the club closes at 6 p.m., there is reason to believe that the witness is lying. Especially noteworthy to our discussion as it pertains to miracle-claims is Richard Givens' observation of how difficult it is to deceive under cross-examination. He writes:

> The wider the angles of divergence between these various images, the more confusing the problem, and the more "higher mathematics" must be done in order to attempt to avoid direct conflicts between these elements. The greater the angle of deception employed, the greater the complexity and the lower the effectiveness of these internal mental operations. If this is conscious, we attribute this to lying. If it is unconscious we lay it to the "bias" of the witness.

> If one is lying or strongly biased, it is not enough to simply dredge up whatever mental trace there may be of the event and attempt to articulate it in answer to a question. Instead, all of the various elements mentioned must be weighed, a decision made as to the best approach, a reply contrived that is expected to be most convincing, and then an effort made to launch this communication into the minds of the audience.

> The person with a wide angle of divergence between what is recalled and the impression sought to be given is thus at an almost helpless disadvantage, especially if confronting a cross-examiner who understands the predicament.

> If the audience includes both a cross-examiner and a tribunal, the number of elements to be considered becomes even greater. The mental gymnastics required rise in geometric proportion to the number of elements involved.[40]

Since the evidence for miracle-claims is not weighed in a court of law, cross-examination comes in the form of empirical investigation and possible counter-evidence. A good analogy to miracle-claims in this respect are the claims associated with the paranormal (such as UFO citings and ghost encounters), some of which have been shown to be fraudulent under the rigors of empirical "cross-examination". Most of the case studies show how difficult it is to *maintain* deception under such investigation.[41]

MIRACLES AND EVIDENCE

Another example of how the rigors of cross-examination can serve to separate the fraudulent miracles from the true ones can be seen in the alleged miracles associated with Mormonism: (1) Joseph Smith's miraculous reception and "translation" of the golden plates of the *Book of Mormon*; (2) fulfilled prophecy; and (3) assorted visitations by angelic beings and Christ himself. Concerning these three alleged cases of the miraculous, it has been pointed out that (1) the *Book of Mormon* has no basis in archaeology, history or anthropology, (2) Mormonism is riddled with false prophecies, and (3) the miraculous supernatural visitations were unconfirmed by other witnesses besides Smith, in addition to being altered and riddled with inconsistencies.[42] Because of this solid counter-evidence, which serves as a cross-examination of the miracle-claims, belief in the Mormon miracles is not rationally warranted. Of course, if Smith's supernatural visitations were confirmed by a good number of witnesses, supported by other circumstantial considerations and his experiences were evidentially inexplicable (although not logically inexplicable) apart from a miraculous interpretation, then a Mormon would be within his epistemic rights in believing that Smith's miraculous tales really happened. Furthermore, the Mormon's case would even be stronger if the *Book of Mormon* was solidly supported by archaeology, history, and anthropology, and Mormonism contained within the writings of its prophets an overwhelming number of fulfilled prophecies. If all this were true, it would form a web of belief which would be difficult to beat.

Let us now turn to the question of the credibility of evidence in situations where indirect, or circumstantial, evidence is emphasized. Wigmore writes that there are three kinds of circumstantial evidence to which an attorney may appeal to in order to demonstrate the actuality of a particular event: *prospectant*, *concomitant*, and *retrospective*.[43] To help the reader know what is meant by these three types of evidence, Windes and Hastings present the following example:

> Judge Alton B. Parker, long-time New York attorney and Democratic candidate for president in 1904, once told of a case he was familiar with that demonstrated the effective use of circumstantial evidence. (The judge strongly believed in the probative value of circumstantial evidence.) The story concerned the judge's first murder case. A defendant was put on trial for killing a woman in upstate New York. Nobody witnessed the killing; there was no direct evidence. In the trial that followed, however, the following facts were brought forth. . .: The defendant bought powder and shot at a local store; he expressed to friends his dislike for the deceased as well as his need for money; he borrowed a shotgun from a resident of the community; for wadding he tore a page from a copy of a magazine subscribed to by the man he borrowed the gun

131

from, using one half of the page for wadding and pocketing the other half; he was seen approaching and leaving the deceased's home on the night of the murder; he tried to spend a five-dollar bill, a counterfeit bill known to belong to the deceased; the wadding was found near the body of the deceased, and the other half found in the defendant's pocket, along with the five-dollar bill he tried to get rid of. From this circumstantial evidence, the man was convicted and hanged. Judge Parker held that such evidence to be conclusive.[44]

We can see the three kinds of circumstantial evidence in the above case: (1) *Prospectant* evidence refers to the motives, attitudes, statements, or actions of an individual which may lead one to suppose that this individual was in the position and was capable of performing the act under question. The fact that the defendant expressed to friends that he disliked the deceased, had a need for money, bought gun powder from a local store, and borrowed a shotgun from a community resident is pretty good indication that the defendant possessed the motive, opportunity, and instruments to perform the murder. (2) *Concomitant* evidence refers to whether certain facts were present which would only be true if the defendant had committed the crime. For example, if the defendant was in California at the time of the crime, or it was equally plausible that someone else could have committed the crime, there would be no concomitant evidence to make it plausible to believe that the defendant is guilty. The fact that he, but no one else, was seen on the night of the murder approaching and leaving the home of the deceased is the concomitant evidence. (3) *Retrospective* evidence looks back at the crime, and on the basis of facts discovered after the event, such as the defendant's behavior and the possession of items whose presence cannot be reasonably explained apart from his guilt, infers that the defendant is guilty beyond a reasonable doubt. In the above case, the wadding both in the defendant's pocket and near the body, and the deceased's counterfeit five-dollar bill found on the defendant's person, make up the retrospective evidence.

After the evidence (whether it is testimonial or circumstantial) for one side is presented at a trial, the other attorney will usually cross-examine the witness or try to impugn the evidence. The jury (whether it be a judge or a panel of the defendant's peers) will then make a judgment as to whether the plaintiff's counsel has sufficiently demonstrated beyond a reasonable doubt the guilt of the defendant. In this sense, legal reasoning is ultimately dependent on human judgment, but it would be wrong to call the process "subjective". For although in the final analysis it is up to the the members of the jury to decide whether or not the evidence is compelling enough to warrant a guilty verdict, it should not be forgotten that legal science provides the jury with some general standards and criteria of evidence, produced by centuries of rigorous application in life and death situations, by which it can come to reasonable conclusions that are not arbitrary.

Let us apply legal reasoning to an example we employed in chapter 6. Suppose that on a particular Sunday, Mrs. D, a person stricken with rheumatoid arthritis for the past ten years, is instantaneously healed of her ailment moments after having been prayed for, in the name of a certain god, by her pastor in the presence of the entire congregation (about 500 people). Given the nature of her illness and the inability for a scientific law to make the healing explicable, this occurrence is a violation of natural law. There is no doubt that Mrs. D had been diagnosed properly. She had been receiving therapy for ten years for a condition which had been getting progressively worse: she had lost the ability to work properly, make a fist, or even grasp her husband's hand. In fact, at times, she could only get along with a wheelchair. And the sleepless nights of body-wrenching pain were almost unbearable. At time t, prior to the prayer, Mrs. D was experiencing all of the above symptoms. At time t_2, moments after the prayer, all of Mrs. D's symptoms had disappeared without a trace of the disease ever having been present. The total and complete vanishing of her illness, and the remarkable fact that her entire bone structure was reconstructed, was later confirmed by a half-dozen awe-struck physicians who had treated Mrs. D scores of times for her arthritic ailment.

In this case, certain circumstantial facts (i.e., indirect evidence, that is, prospectant, concomitant, and retrospective) are verified by expert witnesses. The doctors, who have examined Mrs. D, testify that at time t she was suffering from rheumatoid arthritis and at time t_2 she was not. Her years of therapy and repeated tests subsequent to t_2 verify this healing beyond a reasonable doubt. Those present at the church service, the congregation, Mrs. D's pastor, and her family, testify *directly* to the fact that after the pastor invoked the name of a particular god Mrs. D was able to function like a person not suffering from rheumatoid arthritis. Although one could argue that these witnesses had some vested interest in the actuality of Mrs. D's healing (i.e., their religious beliefs are somehow validated empirically), the lack of obvious internal and external defects in their characters and testimonies, and the inability to explain the event on the basis of counter-evidence (e.g., magician tricks, secret serums, medical deception, or psychosomatic healing), makes such an assertion evidentially implausible. Therefore, even though the skeptic may still want to assert that the event is not a miracle, he has no evidential grounds by which to claim that the theist has no epistemic right to describe the event as such.

NOTES FOR CHAPTER SEVEN

[1]John Warwick Montgomery, *The Law Above the Law* (Minneapolis: Dimension Books, 1975), p. 86.

[2]Russell R. Windes and Arthur Hastings, *Argumentation and Advocacy* (New York: Random House, 1965), p. 116.

[3]*Ibid.* Alan Nevins writes that even when historical evidence "exists with a fair degree of technical integrity, it is not unlikely to be evidence of a type which a keen opposing attorney could riddle with holes." (Alan Nevins, *The Gateway to History* [Garden City, NY: Anchor Books, 1962], p. 180)

[4]John Warwick Montgomery, *Human Rights and Human Dignity* (Grand Rapids, MI: Zondervan, 1986), p. 134.

[5]Stephen Toulmin, *The Uses of Argument* (Cambridge: Cambridge University Press, 1958), p. 7. See also, Stephen Toulmin, Richard Rieke, and Allan Janik, *An Introduction to Reasoning* (New York: Macmillan, 1979)

[6]Bruce N. Waller, *Critical Thinking: Consider the Verdict* (Englewood Cliffs, NJ: Prentice-Hall, 1980), p. 2.

[7]Mortimer Adler, *How to Think About God* (New York: Bantam Books, 1980), p. 150.

[8]*Ibid.*

[9]Hugo Grotius, *The Truth of the Christian Religion*, new ed., ed. Le Clerc, trans. John Clarke (London: William Baynes & Son, 1825)

[10]Sherlock's work is photocopied in *Jurisprudence: A Book of Readings*, ed. John Warwick Montgomery (Strasbourg: International Scholarly Publishers; Orange, CA: Simon Greenleaf School of Law, 1974), pp. 339-459.

[11]For example, J.C.A. Gaskin writes that "'Of Miracles' has strong appearances of being intended, at least in part, as an answer to Sherlock's highly successful, *Tryal of the Witnesses*." (J.C.A. Gaskin, *Hume's Philosophy of Religion* [New York: Macmillan, 1978], p. 108).

[12]Thomas Erskine, *Remarks on the Internal Evidence for the Truth of Revealed Religion*, 7th ed. (Edinburgh: Waugh and Innes, 1823)

[13]This work has received republication in the Appendix of Montgomery's

MIRACLES AND EVIDENCE

Law Above the Law, pp. 91-140, 149-163.

[14]Edmund H. Bennett, *The Four Gospels from a Lawyer's Standpoint* (Boston: Houghton, Mifflin and Company, 1899)

[15]I.H. Linton, *A Lawyer Examines the Bible* (Boston: W.A. Wilde, 1943)

[16]J.N.D. Anderson, *A Lawyer Among the Theologians* (Grand Rapids, MI: Eerdmans, 1973)

[17]J.N.D. Anderson, *Christianity: The Witness of History* (London: Tyndale Press, 1969)

[18]J.N.D. Anderson, *The Evidence for the Resurrection* (London: InterVarsity Fellowship, 1966)

[19]Harvey Cox in "A Dialogue on Christ's Resurrection," *Christianity Today*, 12 (April 1968): 8-9.

[20]For example, Montgomery, *Human Rights and Human Dignity*, pp. 131-160; Montgomery, *The Law Above the Law*, pp. 84-90; John Warwick Montgomery, *Law and Gospel: A Study in Jurisprudence* (Oak Park, IL: Christian Legal Society, 1978), pp. 34-37; John Warwick Montgomery, "The Marxist Approach to Human Rights: Analysis and Critique," *Simon Greenleaf Law Review: A Scholarly Forum Interrelating, Law, Theology, and Human Rights*, 3 (1983-84): 178-183.

[21]For example, John Warwick Montgomery, "Science, Theology, and the Miraculous," in his *Faith Founded on Fact* (New York: Thomas Nelson, 1978), pp. 43-73.

[22]However, Montgomery, in another text, does inquire: "But the issue here is a *miracle*: a resurrection. How much evidence should a reasonable human being require in order to establish such a fact? Could evidence ever justify accepting it?" (Montgomery, *Human Rights and Human Dignity*, p. 154). Unfortunately, Montgomery responds to this inquiry by citing Sherlock's work and stating that Sherlock "is essentially correct that a resurrection does not in principle create any insuperable evidential difficulty. . . In Jesus' case, the sequential order is reversed [i.e., instead of the normal sequence of life then death, a resurrection entails death then life], but that has no epistemological bearing on the weight of evidence required to establish death or life." (*Ibid.*, pp. 154-155).

The problem with this response is that it is simply not realistic. For example, if my next door neighbor tells me that his father passed away last night, that would be sufficient reason in most cases to believe that the event had occurred. On the other hand, if this same

135

neighbor a week later tells me with no additional evidence that his "dead" father came by for dinner that evening, I would be acting reasonably if I did not believe him. I would probably doubt either my neighbor's sanity or the accuracy of his first report (i.e., that his father died). Now if other factors, such as doctors' reports, numerous other witnesses, a missing body, etc., began and continued to converge upon the event, at some point I would have to give up my skepticism in order to remain rational. If this is what Sherlock and Montgomery mean, namely, that miracles cannot be said to admit of no evidence, I have no problem with their reasoning. However, if they are saying that the evidence demanded of miraculous events should be no different than that asked of regular events, I do not see how one can argue anymore for the uniqueness of a miracle.

23That is why Stephen T. Davis believes that he is able to critique this apologetic approach when he writes that a naturalist, who is confronted with a number of well-founded facts which converge upon a miraculous event, would be within his epistemic rights "to begin denying some of the accepted facts. . ." (Stephen T. Davis, "Naturalism and the Resurrection: A Reply to Gary Habermas," *Faith and Philosophy*, 2 [July 1985]: 305).
My point is that to deny facts whose convergence results in the plausibility of believing that a miracle has occurred is to not fully appreciate that our evidential criteria, just as our formulations of natural law, are based on certain regularities and probabilities. Therefore, in terms of the approach I have defended in this book, a naturalist would not be within his epistemic rights in denying these facts (especially if individually each fact does not entail the miraculous, but their convergence does) because he would be giving up the basis by which he argues against the miraculous, namely, the regularity of human experience.

24This summary of legal reasoning is for the most part derived from Windes and Hastings, *Argumentation*, pp. 114-126, and Montgomery, *Human Rights and Human Dignity*, pp. 131-160.

25Windes and Hastings, *Argumentation*, p. 115.

26See also, *United States v. Kauten* (1943), *United States v. Ballard* (1944), *School District of Abington Township, Pa., v. Schempp* (1963), and *United States v. Seeger* (1965).

27Windes and Hastings, *Argumentation*, p. 115.

28*Ibid.*, p. 117.

29*Ibid.*

[30]See Stephen Naylor Thomas, "What is Good Reasoning?" section 2-1 of his *Practical Reasoning in Natural Language*, 3rd ed. (Englewood Cliffs, NJ: Prentice-Hall, 1986), pp. 111-140.

[31]John H. Wigmore, *Treatise on Evidence*, 5 vols. (Boston: Little, Brown and Company, 1904), I: 13.

[32]Windes and Hastings, *Argumentation*, p. 118.

[33]Thomas Starkie, *Evidence*, 1824, Vol. 1, p. 13.

[34]Wigmore, *Treatise*, I: 4.

[35]Windes and Hastings, *Argumentation*, p. 120.

[36]*Ibid.*

[37]*Ibid.*, p. 121.

[38]Patrick L. McCloskey and Ronald L. Schoenberg, *Criminal Law Advocacy*, vol. 5 (New York: Matthew Bender, 1964), para. 12.01[b].

[39]*Ibid.*, para. 12.03.

[40]Richard Givens, *Advocacy*, McGraw-Hill Trial Practice Series (New York: McGraw-Hill, 1980), p. 12.

[41]See the articles in "Part 2: The Argument from Fraud," in *A Skeptic's Handbook of Parapsychology*, ed. Paul Kurtz (Buffalo, NY: Prometheus Books, 1985), pp. 177-358. See also, Antony Flew, ed., *Readings in the Philosophical Problems of Parapsychology* (Buffalo, NY: Prometheus Books, 1987); and Patrick Grim, ed., *Philosophy of Science and the Occult* (Albany, NY: State University of New York Press, 1982).

[42]For greater detail of these alleged miracles and the evidential problems with them, see Walter R. Martin, *The Maze of Mormonism* (Santa Ana, CA: Vision House, 1978), and Jerald and Sandra Tanner, *The Changing World of Mormonism* (Chicago: Moody Press, 1980). Concerning the *Book of Mormon's* lack of archaeological, historical, and anthropological support, I refer the reader to a form letter sent out by the Smithsonian Institute (because of the abundance of mailed questions about the *Book of Mormon* the institute has a standard response), which states that the Mormon text has no scientific support whatsoever.

It is interesting to note that Raymond E. Brown, in his review of the Flew-Habermas debate, points out that Habermas' apologetic technique employed in his defense of Jesus' Resurrection can also be used to show that it is reasonable to believe in the Mormon miracles. From just what was noted in the text, it seems that Brown is unaware of the enormous problems with the Mormon miracle-claims and how these problems cause his analogy to break down. See Raymond E. Brown, review of *Did Jesus Rise From the Dead?* by Gary R. Habermas and Antony Flew, edited by Terry L. Miethe, *International Philosophical Quarterly* 27 (December 1987): 452.

43Windes and Hastings, *Argumentation*, p. 121.

44*Ibid.*, pp. 121-122.

CHAPTER EIGHT

CONCLUSION

Chapter X of David Hume's *Enquiry Concerning Human Understanding*, "Of Miracles," is without a doubt the most influential work written in defense of the position that belief in supernatural occurrences is not reasonable. Using Hume's work as my point of departure, I have tried to answer the two most important epistemological questions asked about the miraculous: (1) Is it ever reasonable to ascribe a divine source to an anomalous event in order to identify it as miraculous?; and (2) What theoretically entails sufficient evidence that a miracle has actually taken place?

Prior to my analysis of Hume's argument, I briefly presented and defended a broad definition of what most religious people generally mean when they call an event miraculous (chapter 2): a miracle is a divine intervention which occurs contrary to the regular course of nature within a significant religious context. Chapters 3 and 4 consisted of a critical examination of Hume's argument. Although there is no doubt that Hume's argument must be seen as an organic whole, it nevertheless consists of two parts. In Part I (discussed in chapter 3), Hume argues *a priori*, concluding that by their very nature miracles cannot be known historically. I call this the *in-principle* argument because Hume is essentially arguing that miracles in principle cannot be known. I concluded that his argument was either question-beginning, confusing the concepts of probability and evidence, or both. Part II (discussed in chapter 4) consists of criteria set up by Hume to judge the historical evidence of miracles alleged to have happened. I call this the *historical-criteria* argument. Although he makes some excellent observations about human credulity and what constitutes good evidence, I nevertheless concluded that Hume's criteria are both logically and epistemologically flawed. Overall, there is no doubt that Hume's argument makes some insightful points concerning the proper skeptical attitude one should have when confronted with miracle-claims, but I do not believe that it succeeds in overturning the possibility that one may have enough evidence to make one's belief in a particular miracle-claim epistemologically reasonable.

Some people argue against the miraculous on the basis that since miracles are defined as acts of God, one must first have evidence of God's existence prior to showing that there is evidence that a miraculous event has occurred. In chapter 5 I argued (1) that the theist is within his epistemic rights in believing in God apart from any evidence, and (2)

139

that there is a cosmological argument which I believe is successful.

In attempting to defend Hume's position in a contemporary context, a number of philosophers have put forth Humean-type arguments. From among these, I chose to deal in chapter 5 with the ones I believe are the strongest, as put forth by the following thinkers: Antony Flew, Alastair McKinnon, and Patrick Nowell-Smith. As with Hume's argument, I concluded that the contemporary arguments are unsuccessful in overturning the possibility of one being within in his epistemic rights in believing that a particular miraculous event has occurred.

Given my negative appraisal of the anti-miraculous position in chapters 2-6, I made some suggestions in chapter 7 as to what direction the believer in miracles may go in showing the historicity of miracle-claims. Hence, in chapters 2-6 (especially in chapters 4 and 5 when I examined part four of Hume's four-part historical criteria) I answered the first epistemological question in the affirmative, and in chapter 7 I answered the second question by showing that it is possible, by employing evidential criteria used in legal reasoning, that one may be within his epistemic rights in believing that a particular miracle has occurred.

BIBLIOGRAPHY

Books

Adler, Mortimer, *How to Think About God*. New York: Bantam Books, 1980.

Anderson, J.N.D. *A Lawyer Among the Theologians*. Grand Rapids, MI: Eerdmans, 1973

Aslup, John. *The Post-Resurrection Appearances of the Gospel Tradition*. Stuttgart: Calwer Verlag, 1975.

Barry, Vincent E., and Soccio, Douglas J. *Practical Logic*. 3rd edition. New York: Holt, Rinehart and Winston, 1988.

Barth, Karl. *Church Dogmatics*. Edited by G.W. Bromiley and T.F. Torrance. 13 volumes. Edinburgh: T. and T. Clark, 1961.

Baum, Robert. *Logic*. 2nd edition. New York: Holt, Rinehart and Winston, 1981.

Beckwith, Francis J. *Baha'i*. Minneapolis: Bethany House, 1985.

Berkeley, George. *A Treatise Concerning the Principles of Human Knowledge*. La Salle, IL: Open Court, 1946.

Brown, Colin. *Miracles and the Critical Mind*. Grand Rapids, MI: Eerdmans, 1984.

Burrill, Donald R., ed. *The Cosmological Argument: A Spectrum of Opinion*. Garden City, NY: Doubleday, 1967.

Carnell, Edward John. *An Introduction to Christian Apologetics: A Philosophical Defense of the Trinitarian-Theistic Faith*. Grand Rapids, MI: Eerdmans, 1948.

Clarke, W. Norris. *The Philosophical Approach to God*. Winston-Salem, NC: Wake Forest University Press, 1979.

Coleman, William L. *Today's Handbook of Bible Times and Customs*. Minneapolis: Bethany House, 1984.

Copi, Irving. *Introduction to Logic.* 5th edition. New York: Macmillan, 1978.

Craig, William Lane. *Apologetics: An Introduction.* Chicago: Moody Press, 1984.

_____. *The Cosmological Argument From Plato to Leibnitz.* Library of Philosophy and Religion Series. New York: Barnes & Noble, 1980.

_____. *The Existence of God and the Beginning of the Universe.* San Bernardino, CA: Here's Life Publishers, 1979.

_____. *The Kalam Cosmological Argument.* Library of Philosophy and Religion Series. New York: Barnes & Noble, 1979.

Davis, Stephen T. *Faith, Skepticism, and Evidence: An Essay in Religious Epistemology.* Canterbury, NJ: Associated University Presses, 1978.

Donnelly, John, ed. *Logical Analysis and Contemporary Theism.* New York: Fordham University Press, 1972.

Dulles, Avery, S.J. *A History of Apologetics.* Philadelphia: Westminster, 1971.

Epstein, Richard A. *The Theory of Gambling and Statistical Logic.* New York: Academic Press, 1967.

Flew, Antony. *David Hume: Philosopher of Moral Science.* Oxford: Basil Blackwell, 1986.

_____, and Habermas, Gary R. *Did Jesus Rise From the Dead?: The Resurrection Debate.* Edited by Terry L. Miethe. New York: Harper & Row, 1987.

_____. *God: A Critical Enquiry.* 2nd edition. LaSalle, IL: Open Court, 1984.

_____. *Hume's Philosophy of Belief.* London: Routledge and Kegan Paul, 1961.

_____, and MacIntyre, Alasdair, eds. *New Essays in Philosophical Theology.* New York: Macmillan, 1955.

_____, ed. *Readings in the Philosophical Problems of Parapsychology.* Buffalo, NY: Prometheus Books, 1987.

BIBLIOGRAPHY

_____. *Thinking Straight*. Buffalo, NY: Prometheus Books, 1975.

Gaskin, J.C.A. *Hume's Philosophy of Religion*. London: Macmillan, 1978.

Geisler, Norman L. *Christian Apologetics*. Grand Rapids, MI: Baker Book House, 1976.

_____. *Miracles and Modern Thought*. Grand Rapids, MI: Zondervan, 1982.

_____, and Anderson, J. Kerby. *Origin Science*. Grand Rapids, MI: Baker Book House, 1987.

_____. *Philosophy of Religion*. Grand Rapids, MI: Zondervan, 1974.

_____, and Corduan, Winfried. *Philosophy of Religion*. 2nd edition. Grand Rapids, MI: Baker Book House, 1988.

Gill, Jerry. *On Knowing God*. Philadelphia: Westminster, 1981.

Givens, Richard. *Advocacy*. McGraw-Hill Trial Practice Series. New York: McGraw-Hill, 1980.

Grant, Michael. *An Historian's Review of the Gospels*. New York: Charles Scribner's Sons, 1977.

Greig, J.Y.T., ed. *The Letters of David Hume*. 2 volumes. Oxford: Clarendon, 1932.

Grim, Patrick, ed. *Philosophy of Science and the Occult*. SUNY Series in Philosophy. Albany, NY: State University of New York Press, 1982.

Gutting, Gary. *Religious Belief and Religious Skepticism*. Notre Dame, IN: University of Notre Dame Press, 1982.

Habermas, Gary R. *Ancient Evidence For the Life of Jesus*. New York: Thomas Nelson, 1984.

_____. *The Resurrection of Jesus*. Lanham, MD: University Press of America, 1980.

_____. *The Resurrection of Jesus: A Rational Inquiry*. Ann Arbor, MI: University Microfilms, 1976.

143

Harvey, A.E. *Jesus and the Constraints of History*. Philadelphia: Westminster, 1982.

Hospers, John. *An Introduction to Philosophical Analysis*. 2nd edition. London: Routledge & Kegan Paul, 1967.

Hume, David. *A Treatise of Human Nature*. 2nd edition. Text revised and notes by P.H. Nidditch. Analytical index by L.A. Selby-Bigge. Oxford: Clarendon, 1978. Reproduction of the 1739-40 edition.

_____. *Enquiries Concerning Human Understanding and Concerning the Principles of Morals*. 3rd edition. Text revised and notes by P.H. Nidditch. Introduction and analytical index by L.A. Selby-Bigge. Oxford: Clarendon, 1975. Reprinted 1777 edition.

_____. *Dialogues Concerning Natural Religion*. Edited and introduction by Norman Kemp Smith. Indianapolis: Bobbs-Merrill, 1947. Originally published in 1779.

_____. *Hume Selections*. Edited by Charles W. Hendel, Jr. New York: Charles Scribner's Sons, 1927.

Hume's Philosophy of Religion. The Sixth James Montgomery Hester Seminar. Lectures by Antony Flew, Donald Livingston, George I. Mavrodes, and David Fate Norton. Winston-Salem, NC: Wake Forest University Press, 1986.

Hummell, Charles E. *The Galileo Connection*. Downers Grove, IL: InterVarsity Press, 1986.

Jurgens, William A., ed. *Faith of the Early Fathers*. 3 volumes. Collegeville, Minn.: The Liturgical Press, 1970.

Kenny, Anthony, ed. *Rationalism, Empiricism, and Idealism: British Academy Lectures on the History of Philosophy*. Oxford: Clarendon, 1986.

Kurtz, Paul, ed. *A Skeptic's Handbook of Parapsychology*. Buffalo, NY: Prometheus Books, 1985.

Laudan, Larry. *Progress and Its Problems: Towards a Theory of Scientific Growth*. Berkeley, CA: University of California Press, 1977.

_____. *Science and Values*. Berkeley, CA: University of California Press, 1984.

BIBLIOGRAPHY

Lewis, C.S. *Miracles*. Great Britain: Fontana Books, 1947.

Livingston, Donald W., and King, James T., eds. *Hume: A Re-evaluation*. New York: Fordham University Press, 1976.

Locke, John. *An Essay Concerning Human Understanding*. Edited by P.H. Nidditch. Oxford: Clarendon, 1975.

_____. *The Reasonableness of Christianity* with *A Discourse on Miracles* and part of *A Third Letter Concerning Toleration*. Edited by I.T. Ramsey. Stanford, CA: Stanford University Press, 1958.

Mackie, J.L. *The Miracle of Theism*. Oxford: Clarendon, 1982.

Martin, Walter R. *The Maze of Mormonism*. Santa Ana, CA: Vision House, 1978.

McCloskey, Patrick L., and Schoenberg, Ronald. *Criminal Law Advocacy*. Volume 5. New York: Matthew Bender, 1964.

McMurrin, Sterling. *The Philosophical Foundations of Mormon Theology*. Salt Lake City: University of Utah Press, 1959.

Merrill, Kenneth R., and Shahan, Robert W., eds. *David Hume: Many-Sided Genius*. Norman, OK: University of Oklahoma Press, 1976.

Middleton, Conyers. *A Free Inquiry into the Miraculous Powers which are Supposed to have Subsisted in the Christian Church, from the Earliest Ages through Several Successive Centuries, To which is Added a Letter from Rome, Shewing Exact Conformity between Popery and Paganism: or the Religion of the Present Romans Derived from their Heathen Ancestors*. London: Sherwood and Co., 1825. Originally published in 1748.

Montgomery, John Warwick. *Human Rights and Human Dignity*. Grand Rapids, MI: Zondervan, 1986.

_____, ed. *Jurisprudence: A Book of Readings*. Strasbourg, France: International Scholarly Publishers; Orange, CA: Simon Greenleaf School of Law, 1974.

_____. *The Law Above the Law*. Minneapolis: Dimension Books, 1975.

_____. *Principalities and Powers*. Minneapolis: Bethany House, 1973.

145

Moreland, J.P. *Scaling the Secular City*. Grand Rapids, MI: Baker Book House, 1987.

Nagel, Ernest. *The Structure of Science*. New York: Harcourt, Brace, 1961.

Nash, Ronald, *Faith & Reason: The Search for Rational Faith*. Grand Rapids, MI: Zondervan, 1988.

Newman, John Henry Cardinal. *Two Essays on Biblical and Ecclesiastical Miracles*. Westminster, MD: Christian Classics, 1969.

Newton-Smith, W.H. *The Rationality of Science*. London: Routledge & Kegan Paul, 1981.

Norton, David Fate. *David Hume: Common-Sense Moralist, Sceptical Metaphysician*. Princeton, NJ: Princeton University Press, 1982.

Pannenberg, Wolfhart. *Jesus--God and Man*. Translated by L.L. Wilkens and D. Priebe. Philadelphia: Westminster, 1968.

Passmore, John. *Hume's Intentions*. Revised edition. New York: Basic Books, 1968.

Perrin, Norman. *The Resurrection According to Matthew, Mark, and Luke*. Philadelphia: Fortress, 1977.

Plantinga, Alvin. *God and Other Minds*. Ithaca, NY: Cornell University Press, 1967.

Popper, Karl. *Conjectures and Refutations*. New York: Harper & Row, 1963.

Price, John V. *David Hume*. New York: Twayne Publishers, 1968.

Putnam, Hilary. *Reason, Truth, and History*. New York: Cambridge University Press, 1981.

Ramm, Bernard. *Varieties of Christian Apologetics: An Introduction to the Christian Philosophy of Religion*. Revised edition. Grand Rapids, MI: Baker Book House, 1961.

Randall, John Herman, Jr. *The Making of the Modern Mind*. New York: Columbia University Press, 1940.

Reid, J.K.S. *Christian Apologetics*. London: Hodder & Stoughton, 1969.

Rowe, William L. *The Cosmological Argument*. Princeton, NJ: Princeton

BIBLIOGRAPHY

University Press, 1975.

Sagan, Carl. *Broca's Brain*. New York: Random House, 1979.

Schaafs, Werner. *Theology, Physics and Miracles*. Washington, D.C.: Cannon Press, 1974.

Smith, Norman Kemp. *The Philosophy of David Hume*. New York: Macmillan, 1941.

Sorabji, Richard. *Time, Creation, and the Continuum*. Ithaca, NY: Cornell University Press, 1983.

Spinoza, Benedict de. *The Chief Works of Benedict de Spinoza*. 2 volumes. Translated by R.H.M. Elwes. London: George Bell and Sons, 1883.

Starkie, Thomas. *Evidence*. Volume 1. 1824.

Stove, D.C. *Probability and Hume's Inductive Skepticism*. Oxford: Clarendon, 1973.

Swinburne, Richard. *The Concept of Miracle*. New York: Macmillan, 1970.

_____, ed. *Miracles*. New York: Macmillan 1989.

Thomas Aquinas. *An Aquinas Reader*. Edited and introduction by Mary T. Clark. Garden City, NY: Image Books, 1972.

_____. *Introduction to Saint Thomas Aquinas*. Edited and introduction by Anton C. Pegis. New York: The Modern Library, 1948.

Thomas, Stephen Naylor. *Practical Reasoning in Natural Language*. 3rd edition. Englewood Cliffs, NJ: Prentice-Hall, 1986.

Toulmin, Stephen. *The Uses of Argument*. Cambridge: Cambridge University Press, 1958.

_____; Rieke, Richard; and Janik, Allan. *An Introduction to Reasoning*. New York: Macmillan, 1979.

Waller, Bruce N. *Critical Thinking: Consider the Verdict*. Englewood Cliffs, NJ: Prentice-Hall, 1980.

Wigmore, John H. *Treatise on Evidence*. 5 Volumes. Boston: Little, Brown and Company, 1904.

147

Wimber, John. *Signs and Wonders and Church Growth*. Placentia, CA: Vineyard Ministries International, 1984.

Windes, Russell R., and Hastings, Arthur. *Argumentation and Advocacy*. New York: Random House, 1965.

Zwart, P.J. *About Time*. Oxford: North Holland Publishing, 1976.

Articles, Papers, and Reviews

Ahern, Dennis M. "Hume on the Evidential Impossibility of Miracles." *Studies in Epistemology*, *APQ* Monograph No. 9, pp. 1-31. Edited by Nicholas Rescher. Oxford: Basil Blackwell, 1975.

Anscombe, G.E.M. "'Whatever Has a Beginning of Existence Must Have a Cause': Hume's Argument Exposed." *Analysis* 34 (April 1974): 145-151.

Basinger, David. "Christian Theism and the Concept of Miracle: Some Epistemological Perplexities." *Southern Journal of Philosophy* 18 (1980): 137-150.

_____. "Miracles as Violations: Some Clarifications." *Southern Journal of Philosophy* 22 (1984): 1-7

Beckwith, Francis J. "Antony Flew on Miracles: A Critique." Paper presented at the Philosophy Graduate Student Lectures. November 6, 1986. Fordham University, Bronx, New York.

_____. "Does Evidence Matter?" *Simon Greenleaf Law Review: A Scholarly Forum of Opinion Interrelating Law, Theology, and Human Rights* 4 (1984-85): 231-235.

_____. "Two Philosophical Problems with the Mormon Concept of God." Paper presented at the 40th annual meeting of the Evangelical Theological Society. November 19, 1988. Wheaton College, Wheaton, Illinois.

Blodgett, Richard. "Our Wild, Weird World of Coincidence." *Reader's Digest* 131 (September 1987)

Bonansea, Bernardino. "The Impossibility of Creation from Eternity According According to St. Bonaventure." *Proceedings of the American Catholic Philosophical Association* 48 (1974): 121-135.

Brown, Raymond E. Review of *Did Jesus Rise From the Dead?*, by Gary R. Habermas and Antony Flew, edited by Terry L. Miethe. *International*

BIBLIOGRAPHY

Philosophical Quarterly 27 (December 1987): 450-452.

Burkholder, Lawrence; Cox, Harvey; and Pannenberg, Wolfhart. "A Dialogue on Christ's Resurrection." *Christianity Today* 12 (April 12, 1968): 5-12.

Camus, Albert. "Absurd Walls." In *Phenomenology and Existentialism*, pp. 489-498. Edited by Robert C. Solomon. Lanham, MD: University Press of America, 1980.

Craig, William Lane. "Colin Brown, *Miracles and the Critical Mind*: A Review Article." *Journal of the Evangelical Theological Society* 27 (December, 1984): 473-485.

_____. "*Creation ex nihilo*." In *Process Theology*, pp. 141-173. Edited by Ronald H. Nash. Grand Rapids, MI: Baker Book House, 1987.

_____. "The Empty Tomb." In *Gospel Perspectives II*. Edited by R.T. France and David Wenham. Sheffield, England: JSOT Press, 1981.

_____. "Philosophical and Scientific Pointers to Creation ex Nihilo." *Journal of the American Scientific Affiliation* 32 (March 1980): 5-13.

_____. "Professor Mackie and the Kalam Cosmological Argument." *Religious Studies* 20 (1985): 367-375.

Davis, Stephen T. "Is It Possible to Know That Jesus Was Raised From the Dead?" *Faith and Philosophy* 1 (April, 1984): 147-159.

_____. "Naturalism and the Resurrection: A Reply to Habermas" *Faith and Philosophy* 2 (July, 1985): 303-308.

Dodd, C.H. "The Appearance of the Risen Christ: An Essay in Form-Criticism of the Gospels." In *More New Testament Studies*, pp. 102-133. Manchester: University of Manchester, 1968.

Flew, Antony. "Miracles." *Encyclopedia of Philosophy*. Volume 5, pp. 346-353. Edited by Paul Edwards. New York: Macmillan & The Free Press, 1967.

_____. "Parapsychology Revisited: Laws, Miracles, and Repeatability." In *Philosophy and Parapsychology*, pp. 263-269. Edited by Jan Ludwig. Buffalo, NY: Prometheus Books, 1978.

149

Gordon, David. "Anscombe on Coming into Existence and Causation." *Analysis* 44 (March 1984): 52-54.

Habermas, Gary. "Knowing That Jesus' Resurrection Occurred: A Response to Davis." *Faith and Philosophy* 2 (July, 1985): 295-302.

_____. "Miracles Revisited: A Reply to Basinger and Basinger." Paper presented at the 39th annual meeting of the Evangelical Theological Society. December 3-5, 1987. Gordon-Conwell Theological Seminary, South Hamilton, Massachusetts.

_____. "Skepticism: Hume." In *Biblical Errancy: An Analysis of Its Philosophical Roots*, pp. 23-49. Edited by Norman L. Geisler. Grand Rapids, MI: Zondervan, 1981.

Hesse, Mary. "Miracles and the Laws of Nature." In *Miracles*. Edited by C.F.D. Moule. London: A.R. Mowbray, 1965.

Hoffman, Joshua. "Comments on 'Miracles and the Laws of Nature'." *Faith and Philosophy* 2 (October, 1985): 347-352.

Hospers, John. "Law." In *Introductory Readings in the Philosophy of Science*, pp. 104-111 Edited by E.D. Klemke, Robert Hollinger, and A. David Kline. Buffalo, NY: Prometheus Books, 1980.

Jessop, T.E. "Some Misunderstandings due to Hume's Employment of the Term 'Reason'." In *Hume*, pp. 35-52. Edited by V.C. Chappell. Modern Studies in Philosophy Series. Notre Dame, IN: University of Notre Dame Press, 1966.

King-Farlow, John. "Historical Insights on Miracles: Babbage, Hume, Aquinas." *International Journal for Philosophy of Religion* 13 (1982): 209-218.

Mavrodes, George. "Miracles and the Laws of Nature." *Faith and Philosophy* 2 (October, 1985): 333-346.

McKinnon, Alastair. "'Miracle' and 'Paradox'." *American Philosophical Quarterly* 4 (October, 1967): 308-314.

Montgomery, John Warwick. "Science, Theology, and the Miraculous." In his *Faith Founded on Fact*, pp. 43-74. New York: Thomas Nelson, 1978.

Nelson, John O. "The Burial and Resurrection of Hume's Essay 'Of Miracles'." *Hume Studies* 12 (April 1986): 57-76.

BIBLIOGRAPHY

Plantinga, Alvin. "Is Belief in God Rational?" In *Rationality and Religious Belief*. Edited by C.F. Delaney. Notre Dame, IN: University of Notre Dame Press, 1979.

_____. "Is Theism Really a Miracle?" *Faith and Philosophy* 3 (April, 1986): 109-134.

_____. "Rationality and Belief in God." In *Contemporary Philosophy of Religion*. Edited by Stephen M. Cahan and David Shatz. New York: Oxford University Press, 1982.

_____. "Reason and Belief in God." In *Faith and Rationality*. Edited by Alvin Plantinga and Nicholas Wolterstorff. Notre Dame, IN: University of Notre Dame Press, 1983.

Roth, Robert J. "Did Peirce Answer Hume on Necessary Connection?" *Review of Metaphysics* 38 (June 1985): 867-880.

Sadowsky, James. Review of *The Kalam Cosmological Argument*, by William Lane Craig. *International Philosophical Quarterly* 21 (June 1981): 222-223.

Sorenson, Roy A. "Hume's Skepticism Concerning Reports of Miracles." *Analysis* 43 (January 1983): 60.

Stein, Robert H. "Was the Tomb Really Empty?" *Journal of the Evangelical Theological Society* 20 (March 1977): 23-29.

Walters, R.S. "Laws of Science and Lawlike Statements." *Encyclopedia of Philosophy*. Volume 4, pp. 410-414. Edited by Paul Edwards. New York: Macmillan & The Free Press, 1967.

Wei, Tan Tai. "Recent Discussions on Miracles." *Sophia (Australia)* 11 (October 1972): 21-28

Dissertations

Beckwith, Francis J. "David Hume's Argument Against Miracles: Contemporary Attempts to Rehabilitate it and a Response." Ph.D. dissertation, Fordham University, November, 1988.

Bilinskyj, Stephen S. "God, Nature, and the Concept of Miracle." Ph.D. dissertation, University of Notre Dame, 1982.

ABOUT THE AUTHOR

Francis J. Beckwith is an Instructor of Philosophy at the University of
Nevada, Las Vegas. He is a graduate of Fordham University (Ph.D. and M.A.
in philosophy), the Simon Greenleaf School of Law (M.A. in apologetics),
and UNLV (B.A.). He is the author of *Baha'i* (Bethany House, 1985), and
articles and reviews which have appeared in *Journal of the Evangelical
Theological Society, Sunstone, Christian Research Journal, Teaching
Philosophy, The Modern Schoolman*, and *Simon Greenleaf Law Review*. Dr.
Beckwith has also taught at Fordham and Clark County Community College
(North Las Vegas, NV).

85077

239.00904
B38